D0017618

# Discovering the Treasure of Marriage

## Debbie L. Cherry, Ph.D.

An Imprint of Cook Communications Ministries, Inc.
Colorado Springs, Colorado

Life Journey® is an imprint of
Cook Communications Ministries, Colorado Springs, CO 80918
Cook Communications, Paris, Ontario
Kingsway Communications, Eastbourne, England

DISCOVERING THE TREASURE OF MARRIAGE
© 2003 by Debbie L. Cherry, Ph.D.

All rights reserved. No part of this book may be reproduced without
written permission, except for brief quotations in books and critical
review. For information, write Cook Communications Ministries, 4050
Lee Vance View, Colorado Springs, CO 80918.

First printing, 2003
Printed in the United States of America
1 2 3 4 5 6 7 8 9 10 Printing/Year 07 06 05 04 03

Senior Editor: Janet Lee
Editor: Susan Martins Miller
Cover and Interior Design: Jeffrey P. Barnes

Unless otherwise noted, Scripture quotations are taken from the *Holy
Bible: New International Version®*, Copyright© 1973, 1978, 1984, by
International Bible Society. Used by permission of Zondervan
Publishing House. All rights reserved.

Library of Congress Cataloging-in-Publication Data

Cherry, Debbie L.
  Discovering the treasure of marriage / Debbie L. Cherry.
    p. cm.
  ISBN 0-7814-3909-4
  1. Spouses--Religious life. 2. Marriage--Religious
aspects--Christianity. I. Title.
  BV4596.M3 .C49 2003
  248.8'44--dc21
                                        2002152155

# Foreword

We live in a fast-paced world that pushes us to do more, produce more, achieve more, and experience more. Every day the pressures of life seem to require more from us than we can give. This fast-paced lifestyle has a profoundly negative effect on our marriages. When we strive constantly to do something new and exciting, eventually we are forced to reprioritize our lives. Since we only have twenty-four hours in a day, eventually something has to give. Unfortunately "new and exciting" almost always wins the priority race, and the "something" that loses far too often becomes our marriages.

When we first meet someone, developing a relationship is the "new and exciting" part of our life, and it takes priority in our thoughts and time—and usually our wallets. Making that other person a priority causes the relationship to grow and develop to a point of falling in love and getting married. But what happens next is something I have seen occur even in my own marriage. The pressures of life, both good and bad, flood in and begin to take over that place of honor and priority. Our marriages can become so deeply buried beneath piles of responsibilities, daily activities, and projects that we forget to give them the daily attention that they need to survive.

I remember a time in my own marriage when I was completely wrapped up in my job and genuinely excited about how busy I was working full time in a church. I would leave the house early for breakfast meetings and come home late after committee meetings. I was rolling and lives were changing, and I felt God must be pleased with me. Then one day I finished with my activities, feeling quite proud of what I accomplished that day. I headed home like any other day, with the expectation that Norma would be just as excited about what I did as I was. But that day I was met with something quite different—a hurt and discouraged wife.

While listening to Norma share her feelings with me that night, I realized that what had become "new and exciting" for me was making her feel ignored and unimportant. I remember saying, "How can you feel unimportant? You're my wife, aren't you? Nothing could ever be more important to me than you!" But it was my actions she was hearing—and they were speaking louder than words.

I learned from that experience that if I wanted Norma to know how very important she was to me, I had to put her and our relationship back in a place of priority. I didn't have a book like "Discovering the Treasure of Marriage" available to me at that time, but I wish I had. In this book, Debbie presents exactly what we need to do to keep our spouses knowing how very important they are to us. She has a fresh and unique way of simplifying the skills needed to keep a marriage growing and strong for a lifetime. Her principals go beyond theory, right to the heart of what we can *do!* Her encouraging way of presenting these topics will bring hope even to a highly damaged relationship. The exercises are practical and are things that each of us should be striving to apply to our marriage every day. The tools she teaches are effective, yet practical and simple enough that I found myself saying, "Well, of course, why didn't I think of that?"

I believe this book, when read and applied, will make a dramatic difference in your marriage. I encourage you to keep it close by and continue to use the exercises for years to come. The result will be a marriage you will treasure.


Sincerely,
Gary Smalley

To Jim,

For your unfailing love, support
and encouragement.

Thank you for your dedication to making
sure I know that I am treasured.

# *Acknowledgments*

Those people who have watched the development of this project know that only one acknowledgment is actually needed here. The chain of events that has resulted in this book being in your hands is nothing short of miraculous. The story is a long one, so for now, suffice it to say that I give all the credit to the wonder-working power of God's hands.

I want to reach down to the bottom of my heart and thank those people who allowed themselves to become a part of God's plan for this book through their encouragement, personal sacrifice and/or active participation:

My loving husband & children: for your constant support and encouragement and your willingness to sacrifice your time with me.

My mother: for reviewing endless pages of endless sentences and trying to make it readable.

To all my encouraging family members and friends: for not giving up on me or this project.

Dr. Wade Goodall: for being the first to strongly encourage me to write.

Erin & Greg Smalley: for being a real "God thing" in my life and for your encouragement and help in getting this book where God wanted it to be.

Sealy Yates and the team at Yates & Yates, Inc.: for being open to an airport meeting, and your willingness to represent a newcomer to this writing thing.

Terry Whalin and the whole team at Cook Communications: for believing in me and in the continued need for a book striving to improve marriages.

All the couples who sat in my office: for sharing your lives with me.

And last, but definitely not least, a huge thank you to Gary Smalley, who has meant more to me in the last year and a half than he could ever know. Thank you for your constant encouragement, for believing God had a plan for this book and for going miles above and beyond to be a part of making that plan become a reality. Your generosity has amazed me over and over.

I pray that the miracles that have surrounded this project will continue as you read this book, and that the final link in this wonderful chain of events will be you and your spouse discovering the treasure in your marriage.

# Table of Contents

# Introduction

What do you think of when you hear the phrase "front row seats"? Well, for me that phrase conjures up images of excitement and honor. Those are the most coveted seats and the hardest to obtain; believe me, I know. Several years ago my husband and I had the chance to see Bill Cosby in concert. He's someone I have always enjoyed listening to and I couldn't wait to get tickets. The idea of front row seats was almost more than I could imagine, but it was worth a try.

I dialed the phone and impatiently pushed my way through all the automated screenings to reach a real person. I knew I would never get a front row seat by simply entering my credit card number into the computer and having it assign me a row. I had to plead my case to a real live, caring, understanding, compassionate, fan-to-the-end kind of person like myself. And finally, there she was on the other end of the phone! "May I help you?" I was off and running, telling her all the reasons I just had to get front row seats to see Mr. Cosby. She listened patiently, empathized appropriately, and tried to politely inform me that there are very few front row seats for sale because most of them are reserved for "special guests" and that usually you have to "know" someone to get these.

"Who's a 'special guest'? I can be a 'special guest'! Just tell me what I have to do!"

As embarrassing as it may be, I have to admit this groveling on my part continued for several more minutes. My desire to have an up-close-and-personal encounter with this star was powerful. The idea of being close enough to see into his eyes and possibly reach out and shake his hand was driving me to the point of begging for even "just one seat?" (Yes, it's true. For a brief moment I had convinced myself that Jim wouldn't mind sitting in Row 34 without me. I was quite pathetic by that point.) As hard as it may be to believe, lowering myself to the point of begging really did pay off in my being granted two front row seats. Well, kind of—front row, balcony.

On the night of the performance, while we waited for the show to begin, I looked down at the people sitting in the front row seats and wondered, *How did they get the privilege of sitting up there? Who did they "know" that gave them that honor? What makes them "special guests"?*

The performance was wonderful, and I was glad just to be in the building, even if I did spend more time watching the big screen than the man himself (and he did seem much smaller in real life—at least from this perspective). However, I couldn't help but wonder how much more exciting it must have been to be sitting in a front row seat. And as I began to feel envious (yes, I know that's wrong) of those "special guests," I was quickly and quietly humbled. God, as He so often does, softly tapped me on the shoulder and whispered in my ear. What He reminded me of that day has never left me. He said (paraphrase by Debbie), "You are a 'special guest', and you do 'know' someone who has granted you the honor and privilege of a front row seat to watch miracles be performed in marriages right in your own office." Wow! And you know what? He was right (not that there was ever any doubt). Because I "know" Jesus Christ personally, I have been given the honor and privilege of having an up-close-and-personal encounter with someone of much more importance than any earthly star. I have been given, right in my own therapy office, a front row seat to watch God work miracles in many marriages. I give myself daily for Him to work and speak through me, and He does. He has taught me through His Word, as well as through my experiences, the techniques you will find throughout this book. He has proved to me over and over that He is in the healing business, and that He wants marriages not just to survive but to thrive. This book is about what I have witnessed and learned from my front row vantage point. In sharing it with you, I hope and pray you will realize that you can have a front row seat encounter with someone who wants to work a miracle in your marriage and to help you experience "happily ever after."

Throughout Scripture God shares His plan for marriage and gives us the basic principals to have a strong, healthy marriage. He teaches us how to treat each other, how we should speak, the importance of listening, how to handle our anger, and so much more. But the statistics continue to indicate that we do not seem to be applying that wisdom to our daily lives. Many research projects, papers, and books have been launched to help explain or deter the number of divorces each year in our society. As the numbers continue to grow, so does the confusion. If the answers are out there, why do people seem to fall out of love so easily? What happens to that blissfully happy couple after their wedding day? What did they lose that had once held them so tightly together? What ever happened to "happily ever after"?

I believe that as couples fall in love, get married, and then begin their lives together, they quickly become overwhelmed with the complexities of everyday life. They lose track of the simplicity of love within their relationship and of the basic concepts that caused them to fall in love in the first place. Once these basics regarding the relationship are lost, the couple then begins to drift apart and feel less connected. If this process continues over time, they will eventually "fall out of love" and likely divorce.

How do we stop this process?

By returning to the basics and learning how to truly "treasure" our spouse. One of my favorite verses is Luke 12:34: "Where your treasure is, there your heart will be also." This verse encompasses our entire lives. You show that you "treasure" something by the way you think and act toward it. The more time and energy you give to something, the more evident it is that you treasure it. According to Luke 12:34, where your time and energy (treasure) are spent, there your heart will be. "Heart" refers to your feelings and emotions. The more time and energy you devote to something, the more positive you are going to feel about it. God understood that our feelings change and result from how we think and act. He knew that we would want to *feel* "in love," and He gave us the key to doing just that. As long as we keep our thoughts and actions toward our spouses focused on the positive, we can experience that "in love" feeling. But as soon as we stop "treasuring" our spouses and stop choosing to spend time and energy focusing on our marriages, then the feelings can begin to change quickly.

This book is based on the basic biblical principal of "treasuring" and will teach you how to apply this principal in all aspects of your marriage. Once you begin to understand the process of falling in and out of love, you will understand that by applying this simple wisdom from Scripture you can remain in love until death parts you. God knew we would make marriage harder than He intended it to be, and that we would put much more emphasis on the emotions than He planned. That's why He gave us wisdom and guidance throughout His Word, and why He taught us the importance of treasuring our marriages.

Keeping a marriage healthy is not as difficult as we make it. Yes, there is something to be said for spending time learning about and gaining a better understanding of the opposite sex—their "cave" or "planet." But let's face it, this understanding alone is not going to improve relationships between men and women. What we need are the skills and behaviors to make each other happy. We knew these skills before the marriage; the problem is we stopped applying them over time. So much of what you need to do you already know. You did it before. Learning a skill again is always easier than learning it the first time.

How many times has your spouse said to you "You seem so different from the person I married"? What happened? Did you really change? Probably. At least some. But what your spouse is really saying is, "You don't do the things for me that you used to do—those things that always made me feel so good." And most likely, your spouse has stopped doing things for you that made you feel good. So both of you feel the other has changed, and you aren't as happy in the relationship as you remember being early on. Reality is that we will all change in our marriages over time. This is due to maturing and life experiences. However, we do not have to change the things we did that caused us to fall in love in the first place.

The basic principles are simply that—basic. Through my years of practice, I have come to realize that what the majority of the couples I work with need is a "Back to Basics" approach. Although the daily workings of any relationship are in themselves quite complex, the *foundation* of a healthy marriage is not. What a marriage is built on will determine its strength. This foundation should be first and foremost Jesus Christ and then the principles taught through Scripture. The focus of this book will be on those foundations and on what made you fall in love in the first place. You will learn how these basic skills can assure that you and your spouse stay in love "happily ever after."

I have watched this process not only in the couples I have counseled, but also within my own marriage. Jim and I started dating when we were young. We dated through high school and college before getting married. During this dating stage, our lives were filled with many positives or "warm fuzzies." We wrote mushy love notes back and forth (we still have boxes full of them), we showered each other with compliments, we laughed together, held hands, and he even opened doors for me. I was convinced that he was practically perfect. Of course he wasn't. And of course, neither was I. During our early years together, we also experienced some negative aspects of our relationship, or "cold pricklies." For example, I absolutely cannot stand to hear someone's teeth on a fork. As far as I'm concerned, that's what God made lips for. But my husband used to do that regularly. While we dated, it drove me crazy, but I was much better at overlooking it because there was so much good—so many warm fuzzies. There were also the occasional disagreements. But of course, even those didn't seem to be any big deal because there were more than enough warm fuzzies to outweigh the minor irritations.

So, what happens to people in this stage of a relationship—where there are many more warm fuzzies than cold pricklies? Where we think and act in very positive ways toward each other? Where we openly "treasure" each other? We fall in love. Our "hearts" attach. We become convinced that the person sitting beside us is the one and only one for us. Well, why not? He or she makes us feel wonderful. We can't wait to be together, and we hang on every word. We don't even care what we do as long as we are together. I was always more than willing to sit and watch Jim work on his car and hand him tools. I didn't mind watching football for hours as long as I got to sit by him and hold his hand. He seemed to enjoy going to the mall and shopping for hours with me. He never seemed impatient, and he was willing to give his opinion (which was always "It looks great on you") when I tried on 20 different dresses that I'm sure all looked alike to him.

How could we not fall in love? We both knew what it took to make the other feel on top of the world. We were treasuring each other like crazy. We actively focused on the positives of the other and told them often how much they meant to us. So, when Jim proposed, there was no doubt I would accept.

We married after college and moved away from our hometown so I could start graduate school. The warm fuzzies continued but at a much slower rate. "Real life" took over. School was demanding for me, and Jim was working long hours to support us. The things we used to do together started taking a back seat to everything else. Jim would ask me to sit with him and hand him tools while he worked on our car, but I would need to study. Or, I would ask him to stay up late and watch a movie, but he was too tired from a long day at work.

There were also those times when stress greatly increased in our lives—such as during finals. It seemed that these were the times that not only were warm fuzzies less evident, but cold pricklies became prominent. During these periods, we just seemed to always be at each other's throats.

I remember driving to school one day after a big argument about nothing in particular and wondering what was wrong. We were still practically newlyweds. Weren't we supposed to be goo-goo over each other? I knew I loved him and believed he loved me too. But what happened to all the good times? Why didn't we feel important to each other anymore? Why did we always seem to fight when we were together?

As I watched our relationship, this theory began to take shape. I noticed we were on an emotional roller coaster with both ups and downs. There were times when we truly enjoyed being together and felt we were back on track. Other times we seemed to really dislike each other. I began to evaluate what led up to these extremes and the answer became clear. The ups were always during times when we made a special and sincere effort to spend time together, give compliments, and make a genuine effort to say how much we meant to each other. The downs, on the other hand, always came after a time when we were overwhelmed by the outside world; we would take each other for granted and even take the stress of our daily lives out on each other. Once we figured this out we became better at staying focused on the positives and giving each other warm fuzzies on a regular basis. We could definitely see and feel the difference.

After seeing this theory at work in my own marriage, I began to apply it in my therapy sessions with couples at all different stages in their lives and marriages. I began to see the power of warm fuzzies in connecting people who had been distant and frustrated for years. They began to grow closer, start liking each other again, and eventually felt their relationship was stronger than ever. Once they felt a sense of connection, they were more able to begin to look at, resolve, and forgive past hurts and cold pricklies without feeling threatened.

Many couples tell me they have been in marital therapy in the past and felt it actually made things worse, not better. They come into my office with great apprehension, but with a sense of desperation. "We have to try something!" We discuss what they focused on in their past therapy, and almost always they describe sessions focused on trying to reduce the negatives in their relationship. They would focus from the very beginning on what they fought about that week, what hurts they were holding onto from the past, or their poor communication and conflict management skills. As I hear this, I begin to see why therapy may have felt like it made things worse.

The skills they learned and the issues they worked on were important and necessary parts of growing a healthy marriage. As a matter of fact, I teach and focus on some of these same issues. However, I do it differently. I feel the order and timing of topics in therapy is most important. Unless I *first* help them learn how to like each other again, they will not feel connected enough to each other and the marriage to work on the negative aspects.

If I begin by focusing on the negative aspects, two things happen. First, I'm not doing my job. I see my job as a therapist as being a catalyst for change. If you bring me into your lives to instigate change and I begin by focusing on the cold pricklies, what change have I produced? You were already focused on all the negatives—and likely *only* on the negatives—of your relationship before you came to see me. My coming in and joining you there does not seem like change to me. Therefore, I would not be doing my job as I see it.

The second thing that can result from focusing on the negatives first is that an already fragile and shaky marriage can actually begin to fall apart completely. The couple has nothing positive to fall back on to give them the desire to work through the hardest parts. Why would you want to go through the painful process of discussing and resolving past hurts with someone you don't even like or see a future with? This is why many couples have experienced therapy as making things worse: not because they had an incompetent therapist or because those skills were not important, but because they did not feel connected or committed. They had nothing to hold them together while dealing with the difficult issues. They would then feel even further apart.

Therefore, I have learned to spend the first several sessions, like the first several chapters in this book, focusing on building up the positives in the marriage. Couples learn or relearn how to identify and express what they like about each other and how to give warm fuzzies. They learn to make each other and the marriage a priority again and not allow it to so easily be put on the back burner. Most importantly, they learn how to treasure each other in their thoughts and actions. Once they accomplish this, the couple has a sense of not only liking each other, but possibly also of "falling in love" again. Their "heart" is back where it belongs. Then, and only then, can they turn to learning the skills to help resolve the negative aspects of their relationship. At this point, dealing with the cold pricklies will not feel as threatening because the warm fuzzies are present. Now they have a relationship that is worth fighting for.

I have taken this same theory and set of skills and presented them in this book. My prayer for each couple who picks up this book and begins to apply the skills presented is that God will bless you and your marriage through each chapter.

# 1

# Happily Ever After
## A Warm Fuzzy Fairy Tale

*O*nce upon a time, Matt and Laura were young and energetic. They had been good friends almost their entire lives. Then one day something miraculous happened.

It seemed like any other day. Matt and Laura were chasing each other around the enchanted lake as they did nearly every afternoon. As Matt rounded the bend just behind Laura, he noticed she had stopped running and was staring at something on the beach. He drew closer and saw a small gold box, partially buried in the sand, glittering in the afternoon sun. The waves splashed against it, washing away residue and exposing more of the beautiful box with each ebb and flow. Matt and Laura knew this part of the beach like the back of their hands and had never seen this box before. Had it just washed ashore?

Curiosity gripped the young couple as they looked first at the box and then at each other. They picked up the box and brushed away the remaining sand. Then they noticed the exquisite, ornate carvings around the sides and top of the box. They knew they must have stumbled upon a marvelous treasure; what else would such a beautiful box be for except to hold a treasure?

As the anticipation grew, Matt and Laura slowly opened the box together. They stared in amazement. Inside this small container were two identical tiny balls of fur and an old, discolored piece of paper. They removed the fragile-looking paper and gently unfolded it. Together they read these words:

This box holds the greatest relationship treasure you will ever find and the most precious gift you could ever give or receive. Although these two balls of fur may be small, they hold within them the power to connect and keep two people together for a lifetime. When exchanged between two people and kept in a place of respect, they will give you many years of happiness. Carry them with you always.

These are your personal WARM FUZZIES.

WARNING:
Do not lose or misplace these warm fuzzies.
If you do, immediate damage to your relationship
is possible. The longer they are missing, the more damage will
occur. Treasure these, and you
and your partner will have the power of love
at your fingertips.

Matt and Laura were confused yet enticed by what they read. How could these tiny balls of fur—warm fuzzies, as the paper called them—hold such power? They knew what love was—at least what they saw in couples around them. But they had no idea where that love started or what kept it going. They had seen several couples start out showing great love toward each other, but over time, love seemed to fade. They had never before understood these mysteries. Now, however, if what they read was true, they held in their hands the answers to that mystery: warm fuzzies.

Dare they?

How could they not try this out?

With nervous anticipation, each reached into the gold treasure box and gently took a warm fuzzy. As they did, an unusual sensation came over them. A slight tingle ran from head to toe. Butterflies fluttered in their stomachs and smiles grew on their faces. What was happening? Each began to feel warm and fuzzy all over. This warming of their hearts was exciting, and they knew they would never want to lose this feeling now that they had experienced it. They decided to keep these warm fuzzies with them at all times and carefully placed them in their pockets. They walked back to their village talking excitedly about the events of the day. When they entered the gates of the village, they went their own ways and spent the evening feeling warm and fuzzy.

The next morning when Laura awoke she immediately reached for her warm fuzzy, which she had placed back in the gold box overnight. What was wrong? Nothing happened. No tingling, no butterflies, not even a smile. She experienced no warmth at all. How could this be? The paper said it would last forever—never run out.

She tried picking it up again, changing hands and shaking it up a bit. Still nothing! She had to find Matt and tell him what was happening.

She ran out of her house and down the street. As she drew closer to Matt's house, she saw him running toward her. Panting and out of breath, he told her that his warm fuzzy wasn't working either. What could be wrong? How could they go on without that wonderful feeling? How could they get it back?

They stood there staring at the warm fuzzies in their hands. Matt asked to see Laura's. She quickly handed it over, hoping he could find out what was wrong and fix it. As she dropped it in his hand, Matt immediately experienced the same sensation that he had the day before. He now knew it could come only from a warm fuzzy.

"It's back! This one is working!" he practically shouted as he handed his warm fuzzy to Laura. She also experienced a sense of warmth all over as she received his warm fuzzy. They smiled and giggled. There was no need to panic. The warm fuzzies weren't broken after all. "Maybe the warm fuzzies just hadn't 'warmed up' yet," they laughed. They again placed the little balls of fur carefully in their pockets and went about the day feeling great!

As morning broke the next day, the unthinkable happened again. This time it was Matt who woke first and discovered that his warm fuzzy wasn't working. He waited a while to see if it just needed more time to warm up. Two hours later there were still no good feelings coming from his trinket. He went looking for Laura. They decided they must have missed something, some key to the workings of these little creatures. So they pulled out the old paper and read the words again:

This box holds the greatest relationship treasure you will ever find and the most precious gift you could ever give or receive. Although these two balls of fur may be very small, they hold within them the power to connect and keep two people together for a lifetime. When exchanged between two people and kept in a place of respect, they will give you many years of happiness. Carry them with you always.

These are your personal WARM FUZZIES.

WARNING:
Do not lose or misplace these warm fuzzies.
If you do, immediate damage to your relationship
is possible. The longer they are missing, the more damage will

occur. Treasure these, and you
and your partner will have the power of love
at your fingertips.

There it was! It was as plain as day. "When exchanged between two people. ..." How could they have missed it? The warm fuzzies weren't working because they had to be exchanged! That's why they had worked again yesterday; they had exchanged them without intending to. Warm fuzzies are so powerful that they make you feel good even when you don't plan to use them.

Once they realized the secret, they quickly exchanged their warm fuzzies and that wonderful feeling returned. They vowed then and there to exchange warm fuzzies every day, even several times a day to keep this feeling between them.

Over the next several months, Matt and Laura made it a priority to take time out of their busy days to exchange warm fuzzies. As they did, they realized that an even stronger feeling seemed to develop between them. They found themselves making excuses to see each other, not just to exchange warm fuzzies, although that was always part of what they did when they were together, but also to just be together. They could sit and talk for hours and hours about nothing. Both felt better when they were together than at any other time. Before long they realized they were falling in love.

As time passed, Matt realized he wanted to spend the rest of his life with Laura. No one had ever made him feel this good. He couldn't imagine living his life without her, so he proposed to Laura one evening as they watched the sun set and exchanged their warm fuzzies. Laura eagerly accepted. She, too, could not fathom her life without Matt.

They married and began a life together that they believed was guaranteed to be blissful. After all, they knew the secret. All they had to do to keep this feeling between them was to continue exchanging warm fuzzies. What could be so hard about that?

They enjoyed their life together. The beautiful gold box had a place of honor beside their bed. They would exchange their warm fuzzies every night before bed and then gently place them in the treasure box for safe keeping overnight. As soon as they woke up the next morning, they would reach for the gold box and exchange warm fuzzies again. They carried the warm fuzzies with them throughout the day and exchanged them as often as possible.

Over time, Matt and Laura's lives became more hectic and demanding. They began to overlook a few of the daily exchanges, but overall Matt and Laura remained connected and close. They shared enough positives through warm fuzzies that they felt good about their relationship. Gradually, fewer and fewer exchanges happened. Sometimes one or the other might forget, but they always tried to remind each other of the treasure held within the gold box.

Then one day when Matt and Laura woke, both started their day without first stopping by the little treasure box. Actually, the entire day went by without a single warm fuzzy exchange. They were so busy and preoccupied with pressures of daily life that they didn't realize what had been missed. Several days later Laura accidentally came across the box buried under a pile of laundry and some papers from Matt's work. She remembered the feeling the warm fuzzies gave and pulled them out to exchange with Matt. As they exchanged them, both were filled with a sense of enjoyment. They remembered the warning on the old piece of paper and pulled it out to read again.

WARNING:
Do not lose or misplace these warm fuzzies.
If you do, immediate damage to your relationship
is possible. The longer they are missing, the more damage will
occur. Treasure these, and you
and your partner will have the power of love
at your fingertips.

They apologized to each other and vowed again not to let these powerful little furballs get lost in the hustle and bustle of their daily lives. They were back on track — briefly. Before long the pressures of everyday life, again, began to take over. Before they even noticed it, the little gold box with its treasure inside had again been pushed aside and buried. Its place of honor was now occupied by their jobs, children, and friends, along with many other "little things." Although these things brought them pleasures, nothing ever felt as good as the warm fuzzies they used to exchange. Matt and Laura found themselves having fewer and fewer good times, and eventually, the warm fuzzy exchanges stopped completely. Without the exchanges, they felt ignored and unimportant. This feeling of being invisible was worse than anything they could have imagined.

Matt and Laura knew they needed at least some exchanges to keep the good feelings between them. When they couldn't find the warm fuzzies, they began to look for other things to exchange. They were desperate for a connection and decided anything would be better than nothing.

One day while Matt searched for something to give Laura that might bring back that warm fuzzy feeling, he saw a small soft ball on the ground. As he picked it up, he noticed its similarity to the warm fuzzy balls he and Laura had found years ago but had now lost. This ball was similar in size and color, but he noticed it was not as soft. He thought it was close enough to substitute for the warm fuzzy and decided to give it to Laura. He truly hoped to make her feel warm and fuzzy again.

He found Laura and handed her his gift. To his surprise, as he gave it to her, the small ball immediately changed. It became cold and prickly, and it actually hurt Laura as she received it. Without even thinking, Laura quickly thrust this cold prickly back at Matt and it also hurt him. Although Matt meant to give a good gift, he realized that neither of them felt warm and fuzzy after this exchange. But they did feel better than when they had no exchanges at all. That feeling of being invisible was gone.

From that point forward, Matt and Laura learned that when they felt ignored or taken for granted, all they needed was some type of an exchange between them. Both preferred a warm fuzzy exchange; but, since their treasure box was missing, the warm fuzzies were not available. During this time they learned how easy it was to find cold pricklies. Now that they were looking, cold pricklies seemed to be everywhere. Had they always been there? Neither of them knew for sure. They had never noticed these small balls, but they had never needed them before. In the past they had been so focused on their warm fuzzies that they had probably just walked right past the cold pricklies. Now, in their desperation, they actually began to look for cold pricklies to give to the each other. The result was almost always to receive another cold prickly in return. They began to store up extra cold pricklies just in case they needed them in the future. They learned that cold pricklies came in all different shapes and sizes. Some cold pricklies even masqueraded as warm fuzzies until they were given away. Matt and Laura became experts on cold pricklies.

Matt and Laura occasionally remembered the gold box that held the key to the love they once felt. They missed those feelings and would start looking for their treasure box. But, before they could find it, they always seemed to come across cold pricklies and would end up exchanging those instead. Then they would forget what they had been searching for in the first place. So the gold box remained buried, and Matt and Laura continued to exchange cold pricklies.

Over the years, alternating between ignoring each other, exchanging imitation warm fuzzies, and exchanging obvious cold pricklies caused Matt and Laura's relationship to suffer tremendous damage. They hardly looked at all like the loving, passionate couple they had once been. As a matter of fact, they didn't even like each other very much.

Then one day, as the whole family was walking along the beach, one of their children looked up and said, "Why did you two get married?" Matt and Laura looked at each other and seemed at a loss for words. Why had they gotten married? What had been so special and wonderful between them so long ago?

And then they remembered!

They sat their children down on the sand and began to tell the story of how they were walking along this very beach many years ago when they found a beautiful gold box. They shared the story about the treasure they had found inside and how they gave each other warm fuzzies almost constantly. They began to smile at recounting these events and began to feel a warmth growing inside. Then Matt recalled the warning on the instruction sheet:

WARNING:
Do not lose or misplace these warm fuzzies.
If you do, immediate damage to your relationship
is possible. The longer they are missing, the more damage will
occur. Treasure these, and you
and your partner will have the power of love
at your fingertips.

He realized they had not taken this warning seriously. They had lost their warm fuzzies and now were experiencing the damaged relationship the warning predicted. They had to stop this destruction. They had to find that little gold box!

They all got up and returned home with a sense of excitement and anticipation. Matt and Laura began to dig through the clutter of their lives, determined to find that treasure. They were careful to ignore the cold pricklies they came across during the search.

Then, there it was!

The gold box that had once held such a place of honor in their home and life was covered with dust, much like it had been covered with sand when they first found it. Together they picked it up slowly and carefully brushed the dust off. It was just as beautiful as it had always been. With much the same feeling as the day they found it on the beach, they carefully opened the lid. They experienced a sense of excitement as they realized that there was hope for this tattered marriage. Maybe they could again experience that love that held them close. They each drew out the warm fuzzies and with smiling faces exchanged them. The feeling was wonderful! Then they exchanged them again and again and again and again and again ... and they lived happily ever after!

# *Beyond the Fairy Tale*

Your marriage is a priceless gift given to you by your Heavenly Father; one that, if treasured, should last a lifetime. So many of us take that gift for granted and do not heed the instructions and commandments given to us through God's Word. And then we wonder why our relationships are falling apart. If we are to protect them from damage, our relationships with our spouses must be second only to a relationship with Jesus Christ. We must keep the positive exchanges and warm fuzzies flowing between us as often as possible.

The warm fuzzies found in the treasure box of your marriage are necessary to keep the relationship strong and happy. They can take various forms. As individuals, we are diverse and have many different needs that work together to form our personal experience of "happiness." Therefore, we would not be happy or satisfied with only one type of warm fuzzy repeated over and over from day to day without change or variety. That would meet only one of our many needs. What about all the others? If the rest of our needs were to remain unfulfilled and ignored, the long-term effects would be unhappiness and dissatisfaction within the marriage. It is essential to be aware of the many needs of your spouse and the different types of warm fuzzies that would adequately meet those needs.

There are almost as many different types of warm fuzzies as there are people to accept them. Although there are general categories of warm fuzzies that nearly every marriage needs, there will also be personal or specific ones that may apply only to your particular relationship. Warm fuzzies can range from quick winks across the room, to sitting down and having an intimate conversation, to knowing how to resolve a disagreement in a respectful manner. The treasure box is also filled with intimate physical encounters, romantic surprises, inside jokes, and fulfilled needs and expectations.

In most relationships, all of the things that fill the treasure box of a content and happy marriage are present either during the dating and courtship phase or the early marital years. Most couples used these treasures in heavy doses during the early years of their relationship when they were falling in love. However, like Matt and

Laura, many of us get caught up in the daily grind and busy schedules and at some point forget to continue to apply these skills. The result is a more distant and less satisfying relationship and eventually, serious damage.

I had a couple in my office as I was beginning to write this book who openly stated their frustration with their marriage and the efforts they had made to improve their relationship. The husband looked at me and said, "Does making each other happy really have to be so complicated? Because if marriage is really that hard to do, then I don't think I want anything to do with it!" My response to him—and now to you—is what this whole book is based on. I believe that keeping a marriage healthy does take time and effort, however it does not necessarily take difficult techniques. Healthy, happy marriages don't require hard work and complicated techniques. What they do require, however, is attention. This book focuses on getting back to basics. What caused you to fall in love in the first place? Why, once you got married, did you stop doing those things that made you feel so good while you were dating? And how do you fall back in love simply by relearning and reapplying those original skills?

Throughout this book, we will examine the different warm fuzzies necessary to keep your marriage growing. Each chapter will focus on a specific type of warm fuzzy and why it is important. At the end of each chapter you will find an application section that will help you apply the skills presented in that chapter. Through these activities, you will learn how to actively use all aspects of the warm fuzzies that fill the treasure box to keep your marriage well-rounded, satisfied, and lasting happily ever after.

# 2

# Warm Fuzzies and Cold Pricklies

## The Key to Staying in Love

*R*eckless words pierce like a sword,
but the tongue of the wise brings healing."
*Proverbs 12:18*

Crying and confused, Lisa sat on the edge of her bed. She and Phil had just argued again. That seemed to be all they did anymore. What had happened to all the fun times? Why did she always feel unimportant and sad?

Lisa vividly recalled their first date and how Phil couldn't seem to take his eyes off her. During their years of dating through college, he seemed truly interested in what she had to say. He was understanding when she was upset, and he would often call her or send a card "just because." They married 10 years ago and enjoyed their newlywed experiences. They used to look forward to their time together. Not anymore. What happened? Where did things go wrong?

Lisa knew adding three children to the equation had definitely affected their ability to be spontaneous and made it difficult to find that all-important time for just the two of them. But did that mean she had to feel miserable? She loved her children and Phil. Why wasn't that showing?

Phil was sitting in the living room with his head in his hands. He, too, wondered what was happening to this relationship with his wife whom he deeply loved. He thought back over their early years together, remembering how she always supported his career, even those necessary long hours. He reminisced about how she showed interest in his day and seemed devoted to him. They enjoyed the same hobbies and activities. They looked forward to being together even when they just stayed home watching sports on TV. Now it was difficult to come home in the evenings. She seldom asked him how his day went. When she did, his response was almost always interrupted by one of the children who would then get Lisa's undivided attention. They never found time for fun anymore, and she told him she didn't even like to watch sports.

About two weeks later, Phil and Lisa were in my office. After 10 years of marriage, they wondered, Is there any love left? What had happened to the romance and closeness they had shared years before? When did it change? They easily recalled the excitement of their dating and courtship. They remembered the late-night walks; the conversations that lasted for hours and hours; the notes, cards, and phone calls "just because;" and the plans they made to grow old together. Now they didn't look forward to seeing each other. They couldn't seem to talk for more than five minutes without arguing. They didn't give cards even for special occasions. They were having difficulty seeing any future together. Their first question to me was: "Can we get it back?"

Can we get "it" back?

What is "it"?

"It" is the magical formula to "happily ever after." It's the instructional booklet that came with your marriage license. What? You didn't get one? Well, maybe that's the problem. Most of us work better when we know the rules. When the instructions are right in front of us we are less likely to skip over the important steps. To our surprise, the most important steps are usually the simplest ones. If we overlook these steps, the repercussions may seem minimal at first, but gradually they begin to snowball. Before long, they are monumental and an avalanche begins.

Where relationships are concerned, the instructional booklet seems to be read thoroughly and used daily in the dating/courtship phase. All the right steps are taken to get your future spouse to fall madly in love with you and agree to marry you. This seemed so easy. Who wouldn't want to live the rest of your life with someone who makes you feel like the most important person in the world? But then, before long, disillusionment comes. The instructional booklet must have gotten placed at the bottom of the pile of daily pressures, children, and careers, or worse yet, lost completely. "Can we get 'it' back?" And if so, how?

The answer is "yes." So now let's focus on the "how," which is based in the theory of Warm Fuzzies and Cold Pricklies.

# How It All Starts

Let's go back in time and see how Phil and Lisa's relationship started to help us better understand what happened.

Phil met Lisa during his sophomore year in college in a general psychology class. He was immediately attracted to her. They began dating, and before he knew it he was thinking about her constantly. He planned his day around when he would see her next. She was intelligent, humorous, and interested in the same things he was interested in. She enjoyed cooking meals for him, staying up late to type his papers, and generally spoiling him. She enjoyed hanging out with him even if they were just studying together. She even enjoyed watching sports with him. He could hardly believe he had found someone so much like himself. He had dated in high school and college but had never clicked with anyone quite like this. He realized he was falling in love.

Lisa remembered meeting Phil for the first time in Psych 101 and was drawn to his outgoing personality. He was easy to talk to and made her feel as if what she had to say was important. He was sensitive enough not to tease her when she became upset about her grades or a fight with her roommate. She remembered him as an incurable romantic who would surprise her with love notes on her windshield, late-night walks in the moonlight, and candlelit dinners. He set aside time in his busy schedule so they could have time alone, even if it was just going to the grocery store. He even liked to go shopping at the mall! She could hardly believe she had found someone so much like herself. She soon realized she was falling in love.

Relationships begin with a time of dating and courtship. This is that stage where we get to know each other. We spend time together talking, laughing, and learning what makes the other person feel good. We treat each other like priceless treasures. This time is full of what I call warm fuzzies.[1] A warm fuzzy is anything you do that makes your partner feel "warm and fuzzy" inside. These are the things that put a smile on your partner's face and warm the heart. When people do things that make us feel important or special, we not only feel good, but we also begin to draw closer. Warm fuzzies include things like winks across the room, pats on the back (both physical and verbal), verbal compliments, and little surprises. Warm fuzzies also include making special time for each other, giving our undivided attention, and anything that nurtures and builds the relationship. We not only tell someone that we think he or she is wonderful, but our actions actually prove it! During those early stages of a relationship, warm fuzzies are abundant. Compliments flow effortlessly from our mouths, and our minds and actions are practically obsessed with making the other person feel great.

Then there are those cold pricklies that are unavoidable, even in this blissful stage. Cold pricklies are those things about your partner that just bug you. They are the irritants within the relationship that you could do without. When present, these behaviors make you feel cold and prickly inside. These are the pet peeves, the personality differences, the occasional arguments (which at this stage are just that—occasional). These are the times when he has to work late and forgets to call, or when she cancels a date at the last minute to go see her grandmother. They may seem minor, but they still hurt.

During this stage of a relationship, when warm fuzzies are more than abundant and cold pricklies seem practically nonexistent, we begin to fall madly in love. We realize that we feel happier when we are with this person than we could have ever imagined. Before we know it we are making plans, first in our heads and then out loud, to spend the rest of our lives together.

So what happens to this seemingly perfect mate? Over time—two weeks, two months, two years, or even longer—things seem to change. We begin to give warm fuzzies less and less frequently. We don't purposefully withhold these from each other. We just simply start allowing everyday life to take over. We get busy. Too busy. We assume that our spouse knows how much we love him or her and how special he or she is to us. After all, we did marry, didn't we? We shouldn't have to give constant reminders ... should we?

Besides, "He should know how great he looks in those blue jeans because I've told him every time he's worn them."

"She should know how much I love her meatloaf because I've told her every time she's fixed it."

"He should know ... ."

"She should know ... ."

Warm fuzzies diminish because we stop giving them and assume the other person "should know." We stop saying them out loud. We may not stop thinking them, at least not right away. But we stop taking the time out of our busy schedules to say them. Then, before we know it, we may even stop thinking about the things we love, admire, and appreciate in our spouse.

The gradual decline of warm fuzzies will be a natural progression in any relationship unless we make a conscious effort to avoid it. But most important, it's a destructive progression. This is what begins the process of falling out of love. Although cold prickles are present in the early stages of the relationship, they are so far outnumbered by the warm fuzzies that they are only very minor irritants. They are easily overlooked because we are focused on the positives. So what happens when the positives occur at a significantly slower rate? The cold prickles become much more noticeable. As the warm fuzzies decrease, they eventually become less evident than the cold prickles; therefore, our focus turns negative. The more we focus on the cold pricklies, the bigger they seem to become. We have started a very destructive snowball effect; and if we are not careful, we will eventually create a full avalanche of marital destruction. Let's take a look at how one woman experienced this move from a positive to a negative impression of her husband simply through a change of focus.

## *The Story of Eve*

As Eve looked around the beautiful garden of her life, she saw blessings and beauty everywhere. Flowers and blossoms of children, a loving husband, a good job, and financial security filled the acres of her life. God had definitely supplied all her needs. He even supplied most of what she could ever want. As she walked around this garden, she focused mainly on the beauty and blessings within. This constant stream of nourishment flowing through her life caused her to barely notice the few weeds that had begun to grow. When she did notice them, she easily plucked them out and wasn't really bothered by them. She knew that no life was perfect, but the irritants seemed minimal.

One day, as she walked through the area of the garden she called her marriage, she noticed an irritant about her husband, Adam, that normally she overlooked. For some reason she stopped before this small tree and stared at it. She knew that this tree of irritation had always been there, and in reality was a very small part of who Adam really was. She usually focused on all the blessings, beauty, and nurturing that flowed from Adam. Today, however, she just stood there before the Tree of Cold Prickles. The longer she stood there and focused on it, the more the tree grew. It grew and grew until that tree of irritations was all she could see. It filled her vision and blocked from view the acres and acres of beauty in the garden of her marriage. She couldn't see the beauty, nourishment, and totally fulfilling nature of the garden as long as she focused on the negative nature of this tree. This ultimately led to more arguments between her and Adam, which caused the tree to grow even bigger. Where had all the beauty gone?

Eventually, Eve made a conscious choice to search for the beauty she knew had once been there. This was not easy, but as she made herself look beyond and around the tree, and actually try to ignore it, she found what she had hoped for—the husband whom God had blessed her with. She was again able to view and appreciate his beauty. And much to her surprise, as she began to refocus on the positives in Adam, the Tree of Cold Pricklies began to wither and fade.

## How Does Eve's Story Apply?

Adam and Eve, like many of the couples I work with, had a relationship filled with beauty and warm fuzzies. They felt blessed and supported by the spouse God had supplied for each of them. Like the Garden of Eden, the marriage seemed perfect and beautiful—fully capable of sustaining Adam and Eve's lives. But in the middle of that garden God placed one seemingly minor irritant and asked them to ignore it. As long as they remained focused on Him and the beauty of His blessings, things went well. But God gave choice to both Adam and Eve—and to our marriages today. Without choice there is no room for obedience, no room for God to prove His love for us, or for us to prove our love for Him and each other. In the Garden of Eden as well as in each of our marriages, there is at least one source of irritation. At least one thing that God is asking us to ignore in order for us to continue to enjoy His blessings. Instead of ignoring this irritant in the garden, however, Eve soon began to focus on it, and her entire mind-set changed. She became focused on the negative and her life, as well as her marriage, suffered.

Many marriages follow this same pattern. We move from being focused on the positives in our spouse and filled with warm fuzzies throughout, to a point where we seem to focus only on the few negatives that are always present in any relationship. As we focus on these cold pricklies, they tend to grow and grow until they are all we can see. We lose sight of where it all began and what we used to like about our spouse. The negatives become all-important and lead us down a road that most of us never want to experience. At its worst, this road can lead right into an attorney's office or to a lifetime of unhappiness. Once on this road, however, there are detours and U-turns available.

Taking these U-turns requires a conscious choice. We must choose to stop staring at the Tree of Cold Pricklies and go in search of warm fuzzies. As we make this turn our mind-set begins to return to the appropriate place, the cold pricklies begin to fade, and beauty is restored to the relationship. The marriage begins to grow again. Our freedom of choice can lead us to marital destruction if we choose to focus on cold pricklies, or to an ever-growing, beautiful marriage if we focus on warm fuzzies and the blessings God has given.

## Where Do You Start?

When people seek to improve their relationships, most of them feel that what they need to do is to reduce the number of negatives or cold pricklies. However, this is not the key. Let me explain. The range for cold pricklies is fairly narrow. There is a maximum amount of stress or negative components we can handle in our lives. In other words, there is a cap or a level that, if we were to exceed it, would likely push us over the edge. This maximum level of stress includes all stress in our lives—work, school, children, marriage, and so on. So, if you have a highly stressful job environment, there is not much room left for stress at home.

At the other end of the continuum, there is no ground zero for cold pricklies. Ground zero refers to place of total void, where no cold pricklies exist. Cold pricklies can be somewhat reduced, but usually not significantly enough to fix the problem. Since we are human and the majority of our lives are spent interacting with other humans, we cannot completely eliminate cold pricklies. I have never met a couple, let alone any person, who has absolutely no stress or negative components in their life. Remember that cold pricklies include any stress or negative interaction with another person. The only way to be totally stress-free is to be totally breath-free! As long as you are alive, you will have at least some cold pricklies in your life.

Now, let's compare this to warm fuzzies. The range for warm fuzzies is infinite. There is no cap. We can never have too many of these. They never lose their power as long as they are given sincerely. We never build up a tolerance to warm fuzzies. They always make us feel good. However, at the other end of the continuum, there is a ground zero. We can experience a total void of warm fuzzies in our life and in marriage. I have actually heard couples say that there is nothing good about their life together.

If your goal is to make a positive change in your relationship, focusing on reducing the arguments, negative comments, and other cold pricklies is not the place to start. You have much more room for change if you first focus on increasing the number of warm fuzzies. What you want is change, right? How is focusing on cold pricklies change? You have already been focused on these negative aspects of your relationship.

If you want change, you must choose to change your focus. You must learn again how to look for and admire the positives in your spouse. Then you must learn again to take the time to convey to your spouse what you like about him or her. You must get back to the place where the warm fuzzies far outnumber the cold pricklies. Once you accomplish this, then you can begin to deal with the cold pricklies. Why would you want to work through a problem with someone you don't even like? The goal is to be sure you start liking each other again—maybe even falling in love again. Then the cold pricklies won't seem so overwhelming and can be more easily resolved.

The ratio of warm fuzzies to cold pricklies is one of the major deciding factors of the satisfaction and emotional depth of a relationship. Beware, a one-to-one ratio (one warm fuzzy to one cold prickly) is not a healthy, exciting, in-love marriage. This one-to-one relationship is no more than a neutral relationship. It would be similar to a relationship with a roommate or sibling. I have often heard couples say things like, "He feels like my big brother," or, "We are great friends, but that's about all," when describing their relationship. These are one-to-one relationships. They are not bad relationships but they are definitely not what most of us desire our marriage to be.

An exciting, strong, and noticeably in-love marriage will have a ten-to-one ratio of warm fuzzies to cold pricklies. To feel that the marriage is "hot," we need to experience many more warm fuzzies than we do cold pricklies. Remember, since we can't make the cold pricklies go completely away, then we must do more than just balance them with the positives. We must far outweigh them with warm fuzzies.

After just a few weeks of focusing on warm fuzzies, you will begin to feel a renewal within your marriage. You will feel you have the strength to work on the cold pricklies. This will not feel as threatening once warm fuzzies have returned. When warm fuzzies are absent, continuing to focus on cold pricklies can be life-threatening to the relationship. However, when warm fuzzies are significantly increased, then the cold pricklies become manageable. Once this is accomplished, you will feel you have the needed commitment to each other to resolve the cold pricklies with skills I will present later in the book.

How long has it been since you thought about the blessings in your spouse? Even more important, how long has it been since you told your spouse what a blessing he or she is to you? What is it about your spouse that truly blessed you recently?

If you do not count your blessings on a regular basis, you become more susceptible to focusing on the weeds in the garden. Once you have focused only on weeds for awhile, you may overlook any beauty that is present. Be prepared as you begin to make a U-turn in your mind-set that it will take some time before these skills are a natural part of your life again.

## Relearning an Old Skill

Be patient with yourself and your spouse. You are embarking on a relearning journey. Although you were once more focused on positives and were able to easily share warm fuzzies, you've lost this skill over time. You'll have setbacks and possible detours as you redevelop these skills. You have been focused on the negatives and participating in destructive patterns of interactions; these patterns will not change overnight.

Trying to stop giving each other cold pricklies is much like trying to stop smoking or overeating. You know the habit is unhealthy, but it's difficult to stop. You work hard to break this destructive habit and may even be successful for a while. Then, under additional stress you slip back into old patterns. This is a normal part of changing old habits. Be patient and willing to try again after a setback. Don't allow these natural detours to run you off track or make you feel there's no hope.

Don't expect perfection. Instead, be persistent and encourage each other. Your spouse is just as frustrated as you are. But as long as you both agree to keep trying, these old skills will become new habits. Give your spouse some slack, and things will go smoother. If you don't, you are likely to discount all the previous efforts and positives when the first setback occurs. You may find yourself saying, "See, I knew you couldn't do it," or, "I thought you would only keep it up for a few weeks. I was right." Instead, prepare for and expect setbacks and be ready to respond with patience and forgiveness. Say, "I know this is hard; let's try again." Remember that it is easier to relearn a skill you once knew than to develop a skill you never had.

Although many of the concepts presented here may just need relearning, some skills will be brand new. The process of learning to apply a new skill is somewhat more time consuming and yet worthy of the effort. Let me take a minute to explain to you the stages you will go through as you learn to apply new skills.

## *Stages of New Skill Acquisition*

Be prepared to experience different levels of comfort as you begin to apply any of the new skills discussed in this book. There are four levels or stages of new skill acquisition you will pass through when learning any new skill. Let me share how Taffeta, my oldest daughter, proceeded through each of these stages as she learned to ride her bike.

The first stage is the information gathering stage. Taffeta had decided she wanted to learn to ride a "big girl" bike like some of her friends. Once the decision was made, we went to at least five different stores (and most of them more than once) in search of the perfect bike with just the right color streamers hanging from the handlebars. Eventually, we made a purchase. This stage also included the time her dad and I spent discussing with her the rules for riding a "big girl" bike. She spent much more time than she wanted listening to the instructions about wearing a helmet, staying on the sidewalk, and how to cross the street safely. Then we talked about what she was supposed to do once she actually got on the bike, and how Daddy would be running beside her holding on to the back of the bike until she was ready to try it alone. Although Mom and Dad were taking this all seriously, it was obvious that her six-year-old mind was not. She stood there impatiently with her hands on her hips and her blue eyes rolling saying "Okay, okay, I already know all that stuff. Let's just go do it!" We knew all she wanted to do was get outside and take off down the street; we also knew that this wasn't going to be as easy as she thought it would be.

This is where you are right now. You have identified a need or desire to learn something new. You are reading this book to learn about new skills to improve your marriage. You are taking the time to get the full set of instructions, although you may feel like you just want to do it now. This is the stage where information is gathered and evaluated.

The second stage is the initial efforts stage. Taffeta decided she had enough information and was ready to try out what she had learned. She began to apply her new knowledge, but with a natural awkwardness that I'm sure she had not expected. She was wobbling and making wide shaky turns to stay balanced. She very often looked back over her shoulder to be sure that her daddy was still there hanging onto the bike. As a matter of fact, she seemed to spend more time looking back than she did looking forward. From the yard I could hear, "Daddy, don't let go! Don't let go!" and, "I'm supposed to do what? This is too hard. I don't think I can do it." These were followed by her daddy's encouraging words and assurance that he wouldn't let go. Eventually, her frustration with not being able to do it the first time (or the second, third, or fourth time) built and she dropped the bike in the driveway and stormed in the house ready to give up. "I'm never going to get it! You can just take that ugly old bike back to the store." After she calmed down, we were able to talk about how hard it can be to learn something new. We reminded her that frustration was normal, but if she really wanted to ride, it would take some practice. We also reminded her how good she was going to look riding that beautiful pink and purple "big girl" bike. A few days later she was ready to try again.

This stage requires lots of support and encouragement to keep from giving up. You will feel awkward and maybe a little silly. It will help tremendously for the two of you to take time to pray and encourage each other on a regular basis, and especially before attempting any of these new exercises. At this stage, you will often refer back to the rules for review and clarification. You may find yourself saying "I'm supposed to do what?" The encouragement you give each other will be invaluable.

The third stage of learning a new skill is the conscious effort stage. In this stage, the skills are well known and beginning to work. "Daddy let go and I kept going!" I heard from a very excited little redhead. Over the next several days Dad just stood in the yard and watched. Taffeta was much less wobbly, but still appeared tense. You could see her concentrating hard on what to do. She was beginning to see the benefit of this new form of transportation, but was still most comfortable staying close to home.

As you enter this stage, you will need very little review, but you may feel you have to constantly remind yourselves to use these new skills. You will begin to see the value and benefits of these skills through the positive effects on the relationship. You may, however, be using the skills mainly in the easier, safer areas for now.

The fourth and final stage is effortless use. At this stage, the new skills become almost second nature. This stage was evident when we watched Taffeta grab her bike, jump on, and take off down the sidewalk without any hesitation. She was yelling at the top of her lungs "I got it. I'm outta here!" She was now able to ride over to a friend's house and out of dad's view. She probably didn't even remember how she got there because she wasn't focused on the skills but on what she would do once she was there.

At this stage you feel assured that you have developed a new habit. You will apply your new skills regularly and without much thought. They will feel natural, comfortable, and almost effortless.

I encourage you to remain patient with yourself and your spouse as you progress through each of these stages with every new skill you learn in this book. Remember that the prize at the end of the struggle is a healthier, happier marriage.

## *Rules of Warm Fuzzies*

It's time to start learning (or relearning) your first skill—warm fuzzies. It may seem unusual to consider having to learn how to give warm fuzzies or that there are rules to apply, especially when you consider how easily they were given during dating and early marriage. No one had to teach you how to melt her heart back then. Why now? Actually, what you are doing is relearning the skills that caused you to fall in love in the first place in order to reverse the falling out of love that has gradually taken over. You are making a U-turn. Believe me, having a road map at this stage will be very useful. That's where the rules for warm fuzzies come into play.

In order for warm fuzzies to be most effective, keep in mind three rules. These rules will ensure that the warm fuzzies are sincere and taken as such. Our society has made light of the power of positive statements by labeling them as brown-nosing or kissing up. This puts a negative, manipulative flavor on warm fuzzies. Instead of being viewed as pure and positive, they are seen as conditional or having strings attached. For example, you compliment your boss and he thinks you are hinting for a raise. Or you tell your coworkers they did a great job and they think, *What does she want?* To overcome some of these negative connotations about compliments, apply the following rules when giving warm fuzzies.

*Rule 1:* If you can't say something nice, don't say anything at all.

In other words, be honest. The Bible says, "An honest answer is like a kiss on the lips" (Proverbs 24:26). Now doesn't that sound like a warm fuzzy!

Honesty is always the best policy; but in the case of restoring marital happiness, it is the only policy that will work. If you can't think of anything nice to say at the moment, it is much better to be silent than to make something up just to make her feel good. Most likely she will know you didn't mean what you said and then you've begun laying a foundation of lies. Warm fuzzies are the starting place for rebuilding and keeping a relationship strong. If the foundation is in any way based on lies, the entire marriage is built on shaky ground.

Be sure that both of you openly state your agreement to Rule 1 as you begin to give warm fuzzies. If you believe your spouse will only give sincere and honest warm fuzzies, then you will start to build trust and a strong foundation.

*Rule 2:* When you receive a warm fuzzy, say "Thank you."

This feedback helps your spouse know that you heard what he or she was trying to say. It shows that you are paying attention and it encourages your spouse to continue doing that behavior. Remembering to say thank you also reduces the chance that you would miss out on a warm fuzzy simply by not attending to it.

Rule 1, regarding honesty, has a big impact on Rule 2. It would be very difficult to say thank you to any statement made by your spouse if you didn't believe it was sincere. What about those statements your spouse makes that are sincere from his or her point of view, but that you struggle to believe? For instance, John sat in my office as we talked about warm fuzzies, shaking his head. I asked him what he was having trouble understanding. His response was one I've heard over and over and usually from husbands. He looked at me and said, "I've tried giving her compliments before; it doesn't work." I asked him to explain.

He went on to say, "I know how much Keri needs to hear compliments to know that I love her. I used to see her smile every time I told her how beautiful she is or how much I appreciate her. But that was a long time ago. Now when I tell her how much I enjoyed the meal she fixed, she just rolls her eyes and says, 'It was nothing big.' Like this morning, before we came here, I told her how great that suit looked on her. I really do think it looks great, but guess how she responded! She turned away and said, 'No, it makes me look fat.' That really hurt me! I felt like she just slapped me in the face, like she was calling me a liar! Why try if she's not going to accept what I say?"

As we discussed this further, we soon realized Keri was not meaning to call John a liar. Actually, she was struggling with her own self-esteem. She didn't believe she looked good, so she had a hard time believing anyone else could think she looked good. She realized then that she was giving John a cold prickly every time she blew off his compliments. She began to work on accepting that John believed what he said, whether or not she did. She was then able to say thank you and became better at allowing the warm fuzzy to sink in.

If you find yourself having difficulty accepting warm fuzzies and allowing them to sink in, you may be struggling with low self-esteem. The importance of a healthy sense of self-esteem in the marital relationship and ways to improve your self-esteem will be addressed in chapter 3. Otherwise, begin right now accepting the warm fuzzies your spouse is passing your way. Keep in mind your joint commitment to Rule 1.

*Rule 3:* A warm fuzzy only counts as a warm fuzzy if the receiver accepts it as one.

It doesn't matter if you intended your comment to be a warm fuzzy. What matters is how your spouse heard it. Often we say things that come across as the opposite of what we intended. We may only become aware of this by the look on the other person's face. We must learn to say things in a way that our spouse can hear them. (More explanation about this will come in chapters 5 and 6 on communication.) If your spouse is not responding with a thank you or other positive response to your warm fuzzy, then you need to reevaluate how you said it. Where warm fuzzies are concerned, the *how* becomes just as important as the *what*.

Let's step into a Friday evening in Ben and Veronica's lives to help illustrate this rule. Veronica has stopped by the beauty salon to have her hair done before going home. Ben takes off early on Fridays and is already home playing with their two children. When Veronica gets home, she is met at the door with smiling faces. Ben immediately notices her hair and says enthusiastically, "Wow, what a hairdo!" Veronica responds with a big smile and "thank you." She feels the extra tip she gave her beautician was definitely worth it and goes to get dressed up for an evening out with her loving husband.

Now, let's take a slightly different look at how this evening may have gone.

It's a Friday evening, and Veronica has stopped by the beauty salon to have her hair done before going home. Ben takes off early on Fridays and is already home playing with their two children. When Veronica gets home, Ben immediately notices her hair and says, "Wow, what a hairdo" in what sounds to Veronica like a sarcastic tone. Veronica responds with a big tear in her eye and would never consider saying thank you. She feels the extra tip she gave her beautician was definitely not worth it and makes plans to change beauticians. She goes to her bedroom and cries. A little while later, Ben comes into the room and is totally surprised by what he sees. He quickly goes over to Veronica and asks, "What's wrong? I told you I liked your hair." To which she responds with more crying.

So what happened? In the first illustration, Ben successfully gave Veronica a warm fuzzy. The only difference between the first and second illustration was the tone of voice with which the statement was made. In the second illustration, Ben may have been just as sincere in his compliment. However, he may have had a very rough day at work, was in the middle of changing the worst messy diaper their six-month-old son had ever had, and had a 3-year-old daughter pulling at his leg, yelling "I want it now!" when he heard the garage door go up. He reminded himself that Veronica had gone to get her hair done and wanted to tell her he liked it if he really did. Veronica then walks in, Ben looks and realizes he does like her hair and in a less-than-enthusiastic voice says, "Wow, what a hairdo."

Although Ben truly did like Veronica's hair, that did not get conveyed to her by the way he said it. Therefore, it did not count as a warm fuzzy. The goal with warm fuzzies is to make sure you make your spouse feel warm and fuzzy when they hear them. If you do not receive a response of thank you, or at least a smile, you can assume he or she did not receive it. You need to try again. Later, you can ask what he or she heard that was different from what you meant. This will help you learn how to say things the next time so that your spouse can hear them as you mean them.

## Application

Now that you better understand the power of warm fuzzies and cold pricklies, you will want to begin using this knowledge. At the end of each chapter you'll find an application section to help you as you begin to apply the skills addressed in that particular chapter. These will be much like the weekly "homework assignments" that I give to the couples I work with.

*1. One Warm Fuzzy Per Day.* Start by focusing on giving at least one warm fuzzy every day. You will find a list at the end of the chapter to get you started. Be sure you follow the rules. You will know your spouse received your warm fuzzy when you hear "thank you." If you don't, you can either assume it didn't come out right, or he or she simply forgot the appropriate response. If it's the first case, then you need to give another one. If the latter seems to be the case, then gently and playfully remind him or her to say thank you. For example, you might say, "That was supposed to be a warm fuzzy," or, "Did you forget to say something?" This usually makes them laugh and then say "thank you."

Warning: Your mind-set can make or break this assignment.

Brad and Linda were on their third marital therapy visit. During the second session I had explained the theory of warm fuzzies and had given the above homework assignment. When they returned, I asked how the past week had gone and if they had given each other the assigned minimum of one warm fuzzy per day. Both said "yes," and then Linda said, "Brad gave me warm fuzzies, but he only did it because you told him to." I think I sighed with as much sadness as Brad did. Not only did Linda miss out on a whole week's worth of warm fuzzies, she ended up actually giving herself a cold prickly.

You will have a decision to make as you begin this assignment. You can either do as Linda did and say to yourself, He or she only said that because Dr. Cherry said to; or, you can hear the warm fuzzy, let it soak in and feel good, and then say to yourself, I'm glad he or she remembered to do what Dr. Cherry suggested. That tells me he or she cares about me and this marriage. Believe me, not every couple that comes to my office—and I'm sure not every couple who reads this book—will actually do this assignment. So if you are one of the lucky ones with a spouse who will agree to apply these new skills, you have two choices. Either miss out on the warm fuzzy all together or end up with double warm fuzzies because you realize they care.

*2. Knee-to-Knee Exercise.* In this exercise, you and your spouse will sit together, knee-to-knee, and bombard each other with warm fuzzies for five minutes. Take turns looking the other in the eyes and saying, "I like it when you ..." or, "I love _____ about you." The other person should respond with "thank you" before giving you a warm fuzzy. Repeat this process for at least five minutes. Don't be surprised if this becomes an emotional time. I have watched many couples in my office moved to tears as they do this activity, especially the first time. The experience of giving and receiving warm fuzzies after any period of time where they have not been present is a powerful one and often brings back a feeling of hope.

The knee-to-knee position is important and will be used in several assignments throughout this book. In this position you sit facing each other with your knees actually touching. This is both practical and symbolic. Eye contact is important and most easily made when you face each other. The knees touching is symbolic of the connection between the two of you. It is safe touch and not too intimate. You will find that you can even argue in this position and still feel a sense of connection. This is also a position where more intimate touch is easily accessible when desired (holding hands or getting a hug). So, pull up a couple of chairs, look each other in the eyes, and sincerely say what you love, admire, and appreciate about your spouse. Then allow your spouse to do the same for you. You should both walk away from this five minutes with a definite warm fuzzy feeling. Enjoy!

# 50 Examples of Warm Fuzzies

"I love you."

"Wow, you look great!"

"I love your smile."

"I really like the way you whistle in the mornings."

A wink across a room.

A hug in the morning.

"You have beautiful eyes."

Give a back rub.

Call in the middle of the day, just to say, "I'm thinking about you."

Leave a love note on her pillow.

"You handled that great!"

"I'm really glad I married you."

"You are a terrific daddy."

"Thank you for praying for me."

"I really appreciate how you manage our money."

"I like that you help out so much around the house."

"That was a great meal."

Meet him at the door with a kiss.

"I missed you today."

"I love the way you take time to read to the kids."

"I really enjoy spending time with you."

Run your fingers through his hair.

"I really appreciate the way you support our family financially; thank you."

"I love that you have such a giving heart."

"I love to hear you play the piano; you're great at it."

"You are a wonderful cook."

"I really like it when you encourage me."

"I like seeing how you are such a great friend to people."

"I love that you are willing to show me your sensitive side."

Set aside time alone, just to talk.

"I'm so proud of you."

"You really are my very best friend."

"Thank you for standing up for me."

"I love the way you keep our home so clean."

"You are a great organizer."

"I feel safe and protected when I'm with you."

"I like that you hold my hand when we are in public."

"I love it when I hear you bragging about me to your friends."

"You are a great lover."

"I appreciate that you take time sexually to be sure I'm pleased."

"I love the way you kiss."

Give a pat as you walk by.

"I like that you ask my opinion about things that don't even involve me."

"I think it's neat that we parent our kids as a team."

"I appreciate that you are good at managing your time."

"You make me feel important to you."

"I love that you remember special occasions and make sure we celebrate them."

"I like that you take time to appreciate the little things in life."

"I think it's great that you are willing to say you're sorry when you mess up."

Turn off the TV when she says she needs to talk to you.

# 3

# *Worth Your Weight in Gold:*

## Learning to Love Yourself

*"F*or you created my inmost being;
you knit me together in my mother's womb.
I praise you because I am fearfully and wonderfully made;
your works are wonderful, I know that full well."
*Psalm 139:13–14*

Get ready. This could be the most challenging and difficult chapter of this book. Right now you might be saying to yourself, "I thought this was a marriage book that was supposed to teach us how better to love each other. Why is there a whole chapter about loving myself? And, besides, isn't self-love a sin?" You may be considering skipping over this chapter to move on to "more important and relevant" information. But I urge you to stay with me and read this chapter through to completion, because one of the first and most valuable warm fuzzies you could ever give to your spouse is learning to love yourself.

You cannot give what you do not possess. Do you believe that statement? A marriage is based on love, commitment, and acceptance of each other. How can someone learn to love and accept another person if he or she cannot first know how to love and accept himself or herself? Let's look at Scripture and see what Jesus says about loving ourselves.

In Matthew 22:34–39 the religious teachers of the time attempted to test Jesus and asked Him which commandment is the greatest. "Jesus replied: 'Love the Lord your God with all your heart and with all your soul and with all your mind.' This is the first and greatest commandment. And the second is like it: 'Love your neighbor as *yourself*'" (emphasis added). That sounds to me like if you don't love yourself, your neighbor has a problem.

## God Doesn't Make Junk

Psalm 139:13–14 declares that we are "fearfully and wonderfully made," and that the works of God's hands are wonderful. If this is true, then why do so many Christians freak out when I tell them that they should love themselves? When I ask them to make a list of wonderful things about themselves, they react as if I am asking them to commit a grievous sin. Many Christians have come to the conclusion that it is wrong to love themselves, and even more wrong to identify openly what they might like about themselves—were they allowed to do so. Heaven forbid they might brag.

I think I know where this thought process comes from. However, more important than where it comes from is the destruction and damage it causes. Scripture says we are to hate evil (Proverbs 8:13; Romans 12:9), or life in this world (John 12:25; Luke 14:26), but not who we are. Instead, the Bible teaches that God values and loves us (Psalm 121; Psalm 149:4; John 3:16); and, that we should love what He has created in us (Psalm 66:1–4; Psalm 100; Ephesians 5:29).

The Bible also teaches us to praise God (Psalm 103:20–22; Psalm 113:1–3; Psalm 150:6) and that we should praise Him for the works of His hands (Psalm 92:1–5; Psalm 138:8; Hebrews 2:7). God expects me to praise Him for the things He has done and the things He has made. I don't think anyone will argue that point. So, if I can stand on a mountaintop looking out over creation and praise God for the beauty of nature, how much more should I be able to praise Him for what He Himself identified as His greatest creation—us?

Look back in the book of Genesis and let's review the week of creation. At the end of each day, God would look at what He had made and evaluate it:

After making the land and sea, He saw it was good (Genesis 1:10).

After making the plants, He saw it was good (1:12).

After making the sun and moon and stars, He saw it was good (1:16–18).

After making the fish and birds, He saw it was good (1:20, 21).

After making the animals, He saw it was good (1:25).

But then on the sixth day, God created man. And at the end of that day, when God evaluated His work, do you know what He saw? It was "very good" (1:31).

Why not brag? God did! Review the verses above. After God did something, He stepped back, evaluated it and gave Himself a compliment: "It is good!" He gave Himself an A+! He liked what He made, and if we are to imitate God (Ephesians 5:1) then shouldn't we also like what He made? When you look at yourself, do you like what you see? What kind of grade are you giving God on His creation? Can you make a list of things you like about yourself? I simply see this as giving credit where credit is due. I can say I like my eyes because I didn't have anything to do with making them look like this. I can say I like that I can write books, because I didn't give myself that talent or the intellect to do it. Identifying the positive things about myself should be nothing more than one more way to glorify God. It's our way of saying we like the works of His hands. It's giving Him an A+.

How it must hurt Him to have His creation say "I don't like what You made, God. I think You could have done better. This looks like something You just threw together at the last minute." He took the time to knit you together in your mother's womb and to count the hairs on your head. Oh, how we must grieve Him when we don't love ourselves.

We are all God-created, and therefore we all have good qualities within us. So many people, however, struggle with seeing the positive traits within themselves and instead see only ugliness and negative aspects of who they are. These are the people who don't like who or what they see when they look in the mirror. They struggle with low self-esteem, and this can be destructive not only to these people, but also to their relationships—especially their marriages.

A person with low self-esteem has a difficult time seeing positive traits in himself or herself and may reach the point of believing there is nothing good to see. Let me use an illustration to help make this more clear.

## *Sunshine Theory*

The positive and good traits of a person are like the sun. They are bright, warm, and beautiful. These are the God-given parts of us, including our physical self, our personality, and our talents. When we feel good about ourselves and experience healthy self-esteem, it's like experiencing a bright sunny day. We can stand here on the Earth and easily see the sun and experience its warmth and its impact on our life and our outlook.

The problems with self-esteem occur when our view of the sun becomes blocked by other things. Several things can negatively impact our sense of self and therefore block our view of the positive qualities we possess. Some of these are anger, depression, anxiety, and experiences of abuse or neglect. When these things enter into our lives, it's like clouds rolling in and beginning to cast shadows. The worse our negative experiences, the darker and thicker the clouds. These clouds can become so thick and dark that they completely block the sun. It can seem like midnight in the middle of the day. And if we didn't know better (and sometimes we don't) we would begin to believe that the sun has actually disappeared. We begin to believe that all our positive traits are gone and have been replaced with blackness. At these times in our lives we most need to have people around us who can lift us up and help us see that the sun is not really gone, but just blocked. The people around us, especially a spouse, have a clearer view of who we really are. Your spouse can stand to the side and see you and your clouds, but he or she can also see what is still there beyond the clouds. Through giving warm fuzzies, he or she can reflect back to you the sun that is being blocked and help you begin to see the sun breaking through the clouds.

You can also help yourself break up the cloud covering by changing the way you think about yourself. Working on focusing on and solidifying who you are in Christ, reading and studying Scriptures that show how much God loves and values you, and realizing you must learn to love yourself before you can adequately love others are all ways to build your self-esteem. Let me give you some specific ways to accomplish this.

# Ten Steps to Building Your Self-Esteem

*1. Learn to use positive self-talk.* The way you talk to yourself has a tremendous impact on the way you feel about yourself. What do you say to yourself when you start your day, make a mistake, or take on a new challenge? Do you call yourself names? Do you tell yourself that anyone with any intelligence could have done better? Do you remind yourself of all the other times you have "screwed up" in the past or started something and not completed it? Are you the kind of person who generally puts yourself down? Or are you the kind of person who can focus on doing it better next time and on what you can learn from what you did last time? Can you give yourself compliments and mean them?

The type of self-talk you use affects your self-esteem. You can't develop a healthy sense of self-esteem if you repeat negative phrases about yourself and your abilities. Negative self-talk usually begins with words like "I can't ..." or "I'll never ..." or "If only I ..." Avoid self-deprecating comments regardless of what part of your life you are talking about (e.g., physical appearance, career, relationships, talents, personality, etc.).

Positive self-talk is simply the act of saying positive things to yourself and focusing on your positive traits. It involves giving yourself compliments and affirming to yourself that you are a lovable, worthwhile, valuable person because God says you are. Just imagine saying these kinds of statements to yourself every day and really allowing yourself to believe them. I'm sure you would agree that you would begin to like yourself more.

*2. Forgive yourself.* God tells us that we are to forgive if we want Him to forgive us (Mark 11:25; Luke 6:37). We usually think of this as forgiving others. But Jesus doesn't specify forgiveness toward others only. He just says to forgive anyone, anything. I believe that refers also to forgiving ourselves. In order for you to begin to improve your self-esteem, you must stop living in the past and reliving your past mistakes. Everyone makes mistakes. The difference between people with low self-esteem and those with healthy self-esteem is what they do with those mistakes. People with low self-esteem are likely to create a plaque commemorating their mistakes. They will hang it on a wall of their mind in a place they pass by frequently so as to be constantly reminded of what a failure they really are. They may even take that plaque off the wall at specific times and beat themselves up with it just for good measure.

On the other hand, people with a healthier sense of personal identity are able to experience a mistake in a much less devastating manner. These people are able to accept that they made a mistake and realize that it doesn't mean they are a failure. They can forgive themselves as God forgives them, and then figure out what lesson they can learn from it and use it to make better choices in the future. The plaque they would hang would be more focused on their attempt or on the lesson learned.

*3. Celebrate your strengths, successes, and talents.* Is it easier for you to recall your past failures or your past successes? When describing yourself, is it easier to come up with your strengths or your weaknesses? Do you acknowledge your own personal talents or are you more likely to focus on what you do not do well? In order to build a healthy sense of self-esteem, you must learn to celebrate your successes, strengths, and talents. So often people can recall a personal failure or most embarrassing moment with great detail and emotion. However, when asked to recall a significant achievement they falter, maybe only stating some brief facts. Make a list of small and large personal achievements, talents, and strengths and review this often. Allow yourself to let it soak in as you consider this positive aspect of yourself. Remember, you didn't give yourself these talents, strengths, or opportunities. All things come to us through the hands of God our Creator.

*4. Give of yourself and to yourself.* The process of giving can lift your spirit faster than just about anything else. When you give "of yourself" you are focusing on what you can do for others. As you give to those around you, you begin to realize that you are useful and have something to offer to others. You begin to feel more valuable—thus enhancing your self-esteem. When you give "to yourself" you are realizing that you are a worthwhile, valuable, and lovable person and that you deserve to be given to. Avoid giving yourself just the leftovers; you deserve the best—indulge and pamper yourself often.

*5. Accept compliments with a "thank you."* Your self-esteem will likely continue to suffer as long as you are not allowing others to give you compliments. As discussed in the last chapter, when people downplay, or even totally reject a compliment given to them, it often is due to their own low self-esteem. Because they don't believe good things about themselves, they cannot believe the compliments handed out to them.

*6. Set realistic goals.* People who struggle with low self-esteem often set goals for themselves that are unrealistic, either in the goal itself or in the amount of time allowed to accomplish it. Or on the other hand, they may not set any goals at all for themselves to avoid the possibility of failure. Both of these situations keep you from experiencing success. If you set no goals, then you can't succeed. If you set unrealistic goals, you set yourself up for failure. Success is impossible and therefore the confidence that comes with success is also out of reach. Success builds self-esteem and therefore we must learn to set ourselves up for success. If you set realistic goals and achieve them, you will like yourself better. Even small accomplishments and daily achievements can give you a boost. Start by evaluating your goals to determine if they are indeed realistic. Then break large goals down into smaller goals and eventually into daily or weekly goals that can be easily accomplished. Record your successes and the completion of these smaller goals to keep yourself motivated and focused on the larger long-term goal. Be willing to start with small goals, and allow yourself to acknowledge these as successes once completed. You will see your confidence and self-esteem begin to grow.

*7. Stop comparing yourself to others.* Much like setting unrealistic goals, comparing yourself to others can cause you to measure your life against unreasonable standards. This will only set you up for failure and continued low self-esteem. People with a negative outlook on life often compare their lives to those who have more, accomplish more, earn more, etc. There will always be people out there who have more than you, no matter how much you have. So if you compare yourself to the Joneses you may eventually catch up and maybe even surpass them. Then what? You notice the Browns have even more yet, and your accomplishments don't really matter because they don't compare to the Browns. It's a never-ending and never-winning battle.

You must learn to live your own life, make your own decisions, and reach for your own goals in order to strengthen your personal self-esteem. You were not created to accomplish what the Joneses or the Browns accomplish. You were created to live your life and accomplish only what God has asked you to do, and to do that to the very best of your ability. If you continue to struggle with a desire to compare yourself to others, try this on for a new perspective: compare yourself only to those who have less than you, because they will always be out there also.

*8. Try new things.* People who struggle with low self-esteem also struggle with a lack of self-confidence. They don't believe in themselves or their abilities and therefore will avoid taking risks or trying new things. If you want to build your self-esteem, push yourself into new areas. Maybe you have always secretly wanted to play an instrument, participate in a sport, learn a foreign language, go back to school, or take a hot air balloon ride. Whatever it is, try it! Simply taking the risk, regardless of the outcome, can increase your self-confidence and desire to try again. Remember to avoid the negative self-talk and comparisons and just have fun.

*9. Associate with and become an encourager.* I think God knew how easy it would be for us to focus on the negative aspects about ourselves and those around us. He also knew the destruction that focus would cause and how much we would need to build each other up. I'm sure that's in part why Scripture tells us over and over to be encouragers and to edify each other. First Thessalonians 5:11 says, "Therefore encourage one another and build each other up ...", and in Hebrews 3:13 we are told to "encourage one another daily."

The types of people we associate with impacts how we feel about ourselves. If you surround yourself with negative people who are constantly saying negative things about you or themselves, you begin to believe and agree with them. However, consider how different you would feel if surrounded by positive, supportive people who build you up, accept you as you are, and encourage you to grow. You will begin to think positively as well, and your self-esteem will grow.

*10. Take control of your feelings.* Feelings are a strong part of who you are. But they should not be the most important part. Often, people with low self-esteem live their lives and make their decisions by how they "feel" at the moment. The problem with this is simple. Due to low self-esteem they are usually feeling down; therefore, their decisions are going to be based on the negative feelings. A vicious cycle has begun that will only confirm the low opinion they already hold of themselves. They end up being controlled by their feelings, which can change at the drop of a hat. To build self-esteem, take control of your feelings instead of allowing your feelings to control you. This next section will tell you how.

# Stop Letting Your "Feelings" Get the Best of You

So often in today's society people base their decision to get married, or even worse, to get out of a marriage, on nothing more than their feelings. They say they feel "in love" or that they have fallen "out of love." They make major decisions based on something that easily changes from day to day or moment to moment. I don't want to discount the importance of emotions in our lives; however, if we understand where feelings come from we can give them appropriate weight in decision making.

God did not give us our feelings and then tell us not to experience them. Scripture identifies several emotions that Jesus experienced and expressed, such as:

Sadness (John 11:35; Matthew 26:37–38)
Anger (Matthew 21:12)
Joy (Luke 10:21)
Compassion (Matthew 14:14; Mark 1:41)
Troubled (John 13:21)
Tired (John 4:6)

Since we know Jesus was without sin, we know the feelings themselves are not wrong. God did, however, tell us to control our actions regardless of how we feel. For example, in Ephesians 4:26, God does not tell us not to feel angry. He does, however, tell us not to sin in our anger. ("In your anger do not sin. Do not let the sun go down while you are still angry.") We are not to act or think in a way that is wrong regardless of how we feel. I think that would mean that regardless of how we feel about our marriage or spouse, we are not to act (e.g., leave the marriage) based on that feeling.

God understands feelings are very real and often very strong. He also knows, however, that feelings never stand alone. In Luke 12:34, Jesus gives us the key to understanding and controlling our feelings when He says, "Where your treasure is, there your heart will be also." Let's take some time to break this verse down to better understand it.

What does it mean to "treasure" something? You show that you treasure something by the way you think and act toward it. The more of your time and energy you give to something, the more evident it is that you consider it to be of high value. When you treasure something, you will not only treat it well, you will also think about it often and in a very positive way. You would not view something as a treasure and then think awful things about it. According to this verse, "where your treasure is" would refer to where you place your time, energy, and thoughts.

"There your heart will be." The heart referenced here does not refer to the physical heart, but rather to our inner self, our feelings and emotions. So if we put this all together what do we get? "Where your treasure is, there your heart will be" loosely paraphrased by Debbie becomes something like: "The more positive time and energy you devote to something, the more positive you are going to feel about it." God knew that our feelings change and are a result of the thoughts and behaviors that have come first. He knew that we would want to feel "in love" with our spouse, so He told us exactly how to do that. For example, when a couple says they are feeling "in love" with each other, that feeling is based totally on the thoughts they have about the other and the behavior they have observed or engaged in. As long as we keep our thoughts and actions toward our spouse focused on the positive, we can experience that "in love" feeling. But as soon as we stop "treasuring" our spouse and stop choosing to spend time and energy focusing on our marriage, then quickly the feelings can begin to change. When you understand that feelings are the result of thoughts and behaviors, you will begin to place less emphasis on the feelings themselves and more on what lies behind the feelings.

Based on the understanding that feelings are nothing more than a result of how we think and act, you will begin to understand that they are not something we can control in and of themselves. We can control our thoughts and actions and, as a by-product, change our feelings. But telling someone to feel a certain feeling is not going to cause it to happen. Have you ever been really sad and had someone tell you to "just snap out of it?" That's ridiculous. We can't just snap into or out of a feeling; we don't have that kind of control. If we did, wouldn't we all go around feeling happy and in love all the time?

Here's a possible point of contention. God commands us to love. In John 13:34 Jesus says, "A new command I give you: Love one another. As I have loved you, so you must love one another." God does not set us up for failure. He would not give a command He knew we could not obey. And if we have established that we cannot control a feeling, then why would God command us to love? Could it be that love is not a feeling? I believe so.

Couples in successful marriages have learned that the love that makes a marriage successful is not a feeling; it is a choice, a decision, and a commitment. It is something we can exert some control over. That "in love" feeling is a result of our choices regarding how we think about our spouse and how we behave toward our spouse. When these thoughts and behaviors are consistent with how we expect people who are "in love" to act, then we feel "in love." However, when the thoughts and behaviors we have toward our spouse are more like those we would expect from people who are not in love, then the result is that we feel "out of love."

In the next section I will explain this further by sharing with you the model I use to help bring these verses to life and show how thoughts and behaviors can control feelings. Understanding this model can actually help hold a marriage together because we can have some control over the outcome. We usually think of feelings in our life as "just happening" to us. We feel that we have no control over them. We don't understand where they come from or how to change or get rid of them if they are negative. For example, you may be going through your day feeling down and depressed. You're not sure why, but you know that's how you feel. Then someone comes up to you and notices your poor mood and says, "Hey, come on, just snap out of it." You know it's not that easy. If you could "just snap out of it" you already would have. So we often think of feelings as having control over us and we begin to make our life decisions based on them. But if you understand the source of your feelings, you learn that you can exert some control over your emotions and, therefore, you gain some power in your life to make decisions and choices that are not based on emotions alone.

# *Rubber Band Model*

I use this model to help people better understand the source of their emotions and how they can have some control over their emotions instead of their emotions controlling them.[1] The model can apply to just about any emotion (i.e., sadness, depression, anger, happiness, etc.). I will use depression first to explain how it works, then we will focus on applying it to the "in love" feelings people think they must experience to remain in a relationship.

The basis of this theory is that we, as human beings, are a lot like a great big rubber band that lies in a nice smooth circle. We like the different parts of ourselves (thoughts, feelings, and behaviors) to be smooth and consistent with each other. In other words, they need to match up and fit together. The verse does not say "where your treasure is, your heart will be far way." It says that where one is the other will be. We also prefer to be relaxed, and we are most comfortable when there is no tension in our lives. The way to avoid tension is to have consistency between our thoughts, feelings, and behaviors.

If you were to place a great big rubber band on the floor, it would just lie there in a smooth circle forever (now that's stable). The only way to make it move is for someone or something to exert some tension on it. We like our lives and our relationships to be stable, although stable may not always mean healthy or satisfying. In order to feel comfortable with yourself and your life these thoughts, feelings, and behaviors need to come together, or match up smoothly with each other.

For example, let's say you feel depressed. This feeling of depression matches thoughts that a depressed person might have ("I'm worthless," "No one likes me, I don't even like me"), and also matches behaviors that a depressed person might have (isolation, sleeping more, crying). When all three of these components come together in a smooth circle, you are in a stable (but in this case, not healthy) state. The rubber band is going to stay right where it is until something changes to add tension and cause it to move.

So how does change occur? By the conscious choice to move one or more of the three points of the circle to a different—hopefully more healthy—space or circle. We have already established that feelings are not something you can change at a whim. Therefore, the "feeling" point on the circle is not the place to start. Feelings will change as a result of thoughts and behaviors changing. If you choose to wait to make changes until you feel like it, then you might never change. When you attempt to make a change in your emotional state, it is the circle that consistently holds two of the points (feelings, thoughts, or behaviors) that will pull the third point towards it (e.g., feelings plus thoughts are stronger than behaviors alone). When you actively "treasure," you are controlling two points: your thoughts and behaviors.

Let's take the depression example again. You have identified that you are in a depression circle and have decided that you no longer want to be in that stable yet unhealthy place. You are aware that there is a happiness circle out there somewhere because you have experienced it in the past, or because you have seen other people who appear happy. You determine to move out of the depression circle and toward the happiness circle. What is your first step? Well, you know that you have to move one or more points of the circle. You are also aware that the feeling point is not a choice. So you decide to focus on changing your behavior.

You move your behavior to the happiness circle by consciously choosing to act in ways a happy person would act (smiling, being around people, talking, etc.), thus causing tension in your stable depressed rubber band. You feel depressed and are thinking depressed thoughts, but you are acting happy. For example, you may have been asked in the past by a group of coworkers to join them for a movie or golf game. Because of your feelings of depression you always declined and went alone instead. Now you decide to make a change in your behavior. You agree to go out the next time you are asked. After all, spending time with friends is a behavior you have witnessed in "happy" people.

Don't forget the rubber band circles. You're trying to move from the depression circle to the happiness circle. Imagine holding the rubber band with two fingers (points) in the depression circle, and then s-t-r-e-t-c-h-i-n-g the third point with your other hand to the happiness circle. Can you feel the tension that causes? It takes energy to make these changes, which is why we prefer to avoid the tension whenever possible. You may be able to maintain this behavior for awhile, but remember, whichever circle holds two points will draw the third toward it. The happiness circle only holds one point (behavior). You focused on changing your behavior even though you didn't feel like it. But your thoughts didn't change. You went out with your friends, but all the while you were thinking to yourself things like, "They don't really like me, they just invited me because they feel sorry for me," and "I don't have anything important to say that anyone would be interested in hearing." So the depression circle still held two of the three points, and would therefore, eventually pull the third point back to its original space.

This process of changing only your behavior and allowing your thoughts to remain in the more negative space is called "faking it." Many of you may have experienced this in your lives. Where you don't really feel like doing something but you know you ought to, so you do it anyway. But even while you are engaging in the healthier behavior, you continue to think negative and unhealthy thoughts. By the end you likely feel worse than before you tried to push yourself.

So, if "faking it" is only going to put you back where you started (or possibly worse), how can you make effective changes? By engaging the principles of "treasuring." You do this by moving not only your behavior to the healthier circle, but also your thoughts. This is much more difficult than just "faking it" because choosing to control and change what we "think" is harder than choosing to change how we "behave." But, for effective change to occur you must make both of these changes at the same time. The conscious choice to control both your thoughts and behavior is the principle called "treasuring." You choose to treasure yourself by knowing that truly happy people not only engage in happy behavior, but also their thinking matches that behavior. If you not only decided to go out with your friends, but also chose to control your thoughts in the process, you would be "treasuring," Instead of negative thoughts, you would focus on things like, "I'm glad they invited me, I'm going to have a good time," or "They must like me, because they keep inviting me to do things with them." Now effective change has begun because you have placed two of the points of your circle in a healthier space. And although this will cause some tension and take some energy, these conscious choices will begin to pull the third point (feelings) toward them. You will gradually begin to feel "happy."

You may already realize how this model of emotions applies to the rise and fall of relationships. Let's look specifically at the rise and extremely quick fall of Michelle and Joe's relationship, and how they used this model to get things back on track.

## They Saw Fireworks

The relationship between Michelle and Joe started with a real bang as they shared their first date on the Fourth of July. They were both in their mid-thirties and had met through a local dating service. Although nervous at their first meeting, they seemed to hit it off immediately, and by the grand finale they were making plans for date number two. The next couple of months were filled with long, late-night talks and as much time together as they could possibly manage. They went hiking, biking, and boating. They enjoyed the same things and loved to hear about each other's workday. Michelle realized that not only was every spare moment shared with Joe, but also every waking (and often sleeping) thought was filled with wonderful and positive thoughts of him. It didn't take long until she began to feel she was in love.

The relationship progressed quickly and they exchanged wedding vows under a sky filled with fireworks the very next year. Neither one doubted their feelings of love. Michelle and Joe both believed these feelings would last forever. However, real life quickly took over. Weekends once filled with fun and games were now filled with laundry, errands, and yard work. Their quiet evenings cuddling and talking on the couch were replaced with one or both of them working late and coming home exhausted and wanting only to sleep. Michelle found herself disappointed with the little time she and Joe spent together. She began to think that he didn't care about her. She also spent time thinking about all the little things she had noticed about Joe that really bothered her. Joe also was becoming more negatively focused in his thoughts about Michelle and actually found himself looking for excuses to work late.

About two months before their first anniversary they had an argument that resulted in Michelle saying she wanted a divorce. She stated that she wasn't in love with Joe anymore and definitely didn't feel happy or satisfied in the marriage. As these words came out, both of them were surprised that things between them had gotten so bad, and how quickly it happened. Although they neither one had a very strong faith, they held beliefs from childhood that divorce was wrong. But didn't God want them to be happy? As they discussed their options, they wisely decided to try marital therapy before seeing an attorney.

When Michelle and Joe entered my office, they both stated that they didn't expect therapy to work, but felt they should give it a try before chucking this relationship less than one year into marriage. They knew they didn't have feelings of love for each other anymore, and they didn't expect to be able to regain them. Michelle stated her confusion regarding divorce as well as her belief that surely God wouldn't expect her to stay in a relationship with someone she wasn't "in love" with, and Joe agreed. It was evident that their relationship was based primarily on feelings, and when those positive feelings of being "in love" disappeared, they were willing to move on in search of more good feelings somewhere else. They did both express a sense of care and concern for the other and didn't want to hurt each other. Michelle even said, "I know I love Joe, but I'm just not 'in love' with him."

I shared the rubber band model with Joe and Michelle. We discussed how they had moved from feeling "in love" to feeling "out of love" as a result of changes in their thoughts and behaviors. We looked at how they had thought and behaved while dating and compared that to how they were thinking and behaving now. Joe was able to identify times when he had been "faking it" as an attempt to make things better. He remembered one night when he came home early to spend an evening with Michelle. The evening seemed to go fine on the outside, but he recalled thinking all night about how he was doing this just to get her off his back about always working so late. He realized he didn't feel any better after the evening was over.

As we continued to talk about how their thoughts and behaviors had affected their feelings of being in love in a very negative way, Joe's face brightened up. He said, "So, if a change in our thoughts and behaviors caused us to feel "out of love," then changing our current thoughts and behaviors could result in us feeling "in love" again, right?" The model was becoming clear to both of them. I shared with them how even their mind-set about coming to therapy would make a difference. If they continued to hold the mind-set of "it's not going to work," then it probably wouldn't. They both committed to holding a more positive mind-set and working on learning to change their thoughts and behaviors in a way that would foster positive feelings toward each other (chapter 4 will explain how). They held on to this commitment, and by the time their first anniversary rolled around they were feeling the spark of their original fireworks returning.

As you see in this example, we can exert some control over our feelings instead of our feelings seemingly controlling us. "In love" feelings are based on positive thoughts and positive behaviors and interactions that occur between two people. "Out of love" feelings can develop between those same two people as a result of negative thoughts and negative interactions. It is not these feelings that we should be basing our relationship decisions on. Instead, the love that keeps a marriage strong begins in the thoughts and behaviors that make up choice and commitment. We must keep focused on that commitment.

## Application

*1. Sunshine List.* Each of us has qualities within us that are good. These are those God-given things about us that often get ignored or discounted when we are struggling with low self-esteem. This exercise is designed to help you identify those things about yourself that are good and make up your "sun." The better your self-esteem, the fewer clouds there will be to block your view of the sun. However, the more you struggle with your self-esteem, the more clouds you will have blocking you and therefore, the more difficult this exercise will be.

Write down one thing every day for 14 days that you like about yourself. Sound easy? Don't fool yourself. This can be quite a struggle for some people. You should write down your positive quality just before going to bed. Then first thing the next morning, you should read your list. If done correctly, you should be reading a slightly longer list of great things about yourself every morning. As you do this for 14 days, you will begin to find that you are developing a more positive view of who you are.

The traits that you identify may come from any of the following categories:

Physical traits: "I like my hair." "I like my eyes." "I like my legs."

Personality traits: "I am compassionate." "I have a good sense of humor." "I am assertive."

Talents: "I am a good cook." "I can play the piano." "I can organize things and people well."

Daily accomplishments: "I was patient with the kids today." "I stood up for myself at work today." "I took time to exercise today."

As you make this list, remember two rules:

*1. No absolutes.* In other words, you can't say "always" or "never" on this list because if you did, you would not put anything on the list. If I had to say, "I'm always a good mom" or "I always like my hair," my piece of paper would be blank. You are not looking for the things that you "always" like about yourself on this list. You are looking for those things you like "on the average ..." "most of the time ..." "usually ..." about yourself.

*2. No "yes, but ..."* That three letter word ("but") is one of the most destructive words in the English language. It discounts whatever came before it. "I really like that dress, but that color's not quite right on you." I don't know about you, but I'm sure not going to want to wear that dress again real soon. "I'm sorry, but ..." "Thank you, but ..." On your list you should not see any "yes, but ..." entries. "I like my hair, but I wish it were red." "I like to sing, but I'm not any good." These comments negate your compliment to yourself. "Yes, but ..." comments may come into your head. Just be sure not to write them on your list.

If you find yourself really struggling with this exercise after one week of trying it on your own, you may ask others for help (especially your spouse). You can ask people to tell you some things they like about you. They have a different vantage point and therefore may be able to see things that the clouds are blocking from your view. Remember however, you can only write down things on your list that you like about yourself. If your spouse says "I really like your smile," and you think, "Yeah, so do I. I just hadn't thought of that," then you can put it on your list. However, if you don't personally agree with what he or she likes about you, then you shouldn't write it down.

Strive to get as many traits on your sunshine list as possible. You can then keep this and read it often (especially on "cloudy" days) to help you remember that you are fearfully and wonderfully made!

*2. Learn to Give God an A+.* If you struggle with loving yourself and developing a healthy self-esteem, spend time developing a list of Scripture passages that help you understand how valuable you really are. Sit down with your Bible and a good concordance and start researching. You may be surprised at how many times God shows us that He values us. He deserves an A+ on creating you.

Here are a few to help get you started:

Genesis 1:26–27
Psalm 8:1–9
Psalm 66:1–4
Psalm 92:1–5
Psalm 100
Psalm 121
Psalm 138:8
Psalm 139:13–14
Psalm 149:4
Hebrews 2:7

# 4

# How Do I T.R.E.A.S.U.R.E. Thee? Let Me Count the Ways.

## The Art of Treasuring Your Spouse

*F*or where your treasure is, there your heart will be also.
*Luke 12:34*

Remember Matt and Laura from the fairy tale in chapter 1? When they found the treasure box that held the warm fuzzies — and then realized just how valuable this find really was — they were careful to take very good care of it. At least for awhile. They gave it a place of honor in their home and held it gently in their hands every day. They kept it dusted and polished, and they cared for it as a cherished possession. But after awhile, they found themselves taking it for granted — completely disregarding it at times.

After ignoring the treasure box for a while, Matt and Laura experienced damage to their relationship and a feeling of growing apart. They spent less time together, and what time they did have together was much less satisfying than in the past. Before long all they thought about were the negative aspects of each other. They felt like they had fallen out of love. They even considered ending their relationship at one point.

Then they remembered the treasure box and searched until they found it. They began doing the things they used to do—exchanging warm fuzzies. They focused on the positive aspects of the marriage. Matt and Laura realized that it wasn't the treasure box or what it held that was priceless. The true treasure was a happy marriage. They realized that when they kept doing the things they had learned from the treasure box and kept thinking positively about each other, a happy and satisfying relationship resulted. However, when they stopped doing those things, their thoughts turned negative and the result was a relationship they considered casting into the sea.

In "commanding" us to love one another, God shows us that love is not a feeling we can't control. He would not command us to do something we can't do. Love is a choice based on thoughts and behaviors we can control. The act of "treasuring" your spouse is directly related to the rubber band model discussed in the previous chapter. When you choose to treasure your spouse, you will fill your mind with positive thoughts. Your behavior will also be positive and focused on helping and protecting. This chapter focuses on specific ways to keep your thoughts and behaviors in the "in love" circle so that you will continue to feel "in love."

## The Art of Treasuring Your Spouse

Have you treasured an object? A trophy, a prize, a car, or a house? How do we treat an important object? Do we toss it in the closet and ignore it? Of course not. Usually we display it in a place of honor and keep it well cared for. We think about it often and tell others about it whenever we can.

I remember finally finding the perfect house after six months of searching. Finding that house felt like finding a hidden treasure. Over the next several weeks practically all I could talk about was the house. I spent hours and hours thinking about it and decorating it in my head. When it was actually ours, I spent hours and hours actually decorating! I continued to take pride in the house and enjoyed showing it off to friends and family as long as we lived there.

I'm sure most of you can relate to some object in your life that took a place of honor in your heart. Maybe it was that car you wanted for so long and washed everyday, or that medal you proudly displayed, or that trophy bass that you had mounted so you could show it off. Why do we so often take better care of our material possessions than our spouses? Unfortunately, I have to admit at times I took better care of my home than I did my husband. Maybe this is because we are taught how to clean house, wash a car, or take care of things we own, but often we are not taught how to treasure people. This section of the book is devoted to teaching you how to treasure your spouse. It will include treasuring in both thoughts and behaviors, which will help develop and sustain a healthy, happy marriage. Only when we truly learn to treasure our spouse above and beyond anything else (except our relationship with God) will our marriages begin to heal, grow, and blossom.

## How to T.R.E.A.S.U.R.E. Your Spouse

What does it mean to treasure something? It simply means to view that thing as being of great value to you. Something that you dreamed of, worked for, and finally received. A priceless gift. A treasure. Something you are thankful for and never take for granted. Something that you take care of, protect, and pamper. Obviously we should treat our spouse better than any material possession. But do we even know how? We take good care of our car, house, boat, or our precious trophy or medal. But we have a much more valuable gift that we often treat with little concern—a spouse.

Have you ever walked into someone's home or gone to a garage sale and seen an antique table or a limited edition baseball card or other collectible being sold for practically nothing? Or maybe worse, something valuable sat in a corner and was used as a child's coloring table. Maybe it was covered with dust, chipped and scratched, tattered and worn. You look at that valuable object and think to yourself, "These people must have no idea what they have or they wouldn't be treating it like that." I think it's often like that with our spouse. We lose track of his or her value. We seem unaware of how much our spouse is really worth. We need to learn what it means to truly treasure our spouse and start applying these skills immediately!

**T.R.E.A.S.U.R.E.**
**T: Think Positively**
**R: Respect Your Spouse**
**E: Enjoy**
**A: Attend**
**S: Shield**
**U: Understand**
**R: Romance**
**E: Edify**

Let's look at the components that make up T.R.E.A.S.U.R.E.

# *T*

## *Think Positively*

> Finally brothers, whatever is true, whatever is noble, whatever is right, whatever is pure, whatever is lovely, whatever is admirable—if anything is excellent or praiseworthy—think about such things.
> *Philippians 4:8*

Remember the "Story of Eve" and the "Tree of Irritation" from chapter 2? That story explained that what we choose to focus on is accentuated and can become practically all that we see. In order to truly treasure something (or someone!) we must have positive thoughts about it. Can you imagine saying you treasure something but then only considering the negative aspects? A few years ago at the summer Olympics, one particular athlete, a swimmer, was expected to win multiple medals. After winning two gold medals, he was set for race number three. The end result, however, was not another gold medal. The commentators and the interviewers focused on the race he lost rather than the several he ended up winning. I wonder how that athlete responded once he got home? Did he proudly display his medals and view them as a treasure he wanted to show off? Did he have positive memories every time he passed by them? Or did he instead focus on the negative, like the commentators? Did he allow those medals to remind him only of what he lost and the mistakes he may have made?

To treasure your spouse, focus your thoughts on his or her positive traits and strengths. Selectively ignore the negative characteristics and weaknesses of your spouse. God tells us in Philippians 4:8 to keep our thoughts on things that are pure, lovely, and admirable. At no point do I see Him telling us to think on the negative, ugly, and irritating. Therefore it would seem that He wants us to actively avoid thinking about things that are negative. Applying this principle will increase happiness in marriage. Research shows that "happy couples are couples that accentuate the partner's good traits and motives as causes of his or her positive behavior; his or her negative behavior is seen as rare and unintentional or situational. The happy spouse, thereby, reinforces his or her partner's good traits. In contrast, unhappy couples overlook the positive and emphasize the partner's bad personality traits and negative attitudes as the causes of marital problems."[1]

# R

*Respect Your Spouse*

Show proper respect to everyone.
*1 Peter 2:17*

"I just want to be respected." We have probably all said that at one time or another. And we have heard others say it. Respect can be a hard word to define, and even harder to identify in specific behavior. Let's go to the dictionary. In Webster's Dictionary, respect is defined as "to hold in high esteem, honor or reverence; to treat with consideration."[2] Wow, what a definition. How do you think your spouse would feel if you applied that definition every day? Truly treasured.

Showing respect for your spouse means giving the absolute best part of yourself: the best of your attitude, your time, your language, your dress, your gifts—the best everything. So often our spouses end up getting our leftovers, not our best. Do you treat your spouse as well as you would treat a casual acquaintance or even a stranger? If you are like many of us, probably not. It's pretty sad that we would show more consideration to a stranger than to a spouse. Treasuring means treating your spouse as well as you would the president of the United States, the queen of England, Billy Graham, or whoever it is you greatly admire.

Let's say you've had a really rotten day at work, got stuck in traffic for an hour, and are generally in a very bad mood by the time you reach home. Then, as you walk into your house, an old friend you completely forgot was coming for dinner greets you. Let's say that old friend is none other than Jesus Christ. I can see it now. The frown on the face and the growl in the voice would quickly be replaced with a smile and pleasantries. You would do your best to put the bad day behind you. You would likely give Jesus a hug and tell Him how much you have missed Him and how glad you are to see Him. How likely is it that your spouse would have received that same type of greeting from you after the same kind of day? If you're like most of us, it's probably not very likely. But that is what we should strive for. We can talk about a bad day without taking it out on the ones we love.

Be sure your spouse gets your best. Show respect in all you say and do. Be sure the way you talk to—or about—your spouse is honoring and considerate. Don't use hurtful or rough language with your spouse, and don't tease about sensitive topics. Show respect for their need for both individuality and togetherness and help to keep these balanced.

*Enjoy your spouse*

May your fountain be blessed, and may you rejoice
in the wife (husband) of your youth.
*Proverbs 5:18*

Here comes the importance of being best friends with your spouse. Build the friendship part of your relationship by sharing experiences together. Actively set aside time to be together and protect these times. Don't hesitate to pencil your spouse into your daily calendar. After all, you put all your other important meetings and appointments in there. Fill your time together with talking, laughing, and playing. Find specific recreational activities you both enjoy. (See the application section of this chapter for help with developing a list of things you could do together.)

Pleasure and laughter build a foundation of emotional safety, which is essential to a marriage. Focus on finding pleasure in all that you do. Do you remember when you were young how, no matter what you had to do, it was more fun to do it with your best friend? Why not apply this now to your spouse? Do anything you possibly can together. You can make even the mundane things more fun if you do them together. Wash the dishes and put bubbles on her nose or grab hands in the water. Have a pillow fight before making the bed. Rake the leaves and then jump in. Be sure to find fun and laughter everywhere you can.

*Attend to your spouse*

Guard what has been entrusted to your care.
*1 Timothy 6:20*

Remember the treasured trophy, car, or house? Once you acquire these, do you put them away and ignore them? Probably not. But our spouses may feel at times as if they have been placed on a shelf and forgotten. We are born with an extremely high need for attention. Although this may reduce somewhat over time, we never outgrow it.

I often teach parents of young children that their most powerful and effective parenting tool is their attention. Those behaviors that they attend to in their child are the behaviors that are being reinforced and therefore will be repeated. And the behaviors they ignore are not reinforced and therefore begin to decline. Their child's "job" is to soak up as much attention as possible. Children hate being ignored because it means they are not doing their job. Children who are ignored for extended amounts of time will begin looking for ways—positive or negative—to get attention.

What's interesting about this is that the same theory holds true as adults. We never outgrow our desire to soak up as much attention as possible and, therefore, one of the strongest and most effective skills to keeping a marriage strong is to give our spouse attention. You have two types of attention to give—positive and negative. Whatever you attend to (either positively or negatively) will be reinforced. If you give your spouse positive attention (hugs, thank yous, time to cuddle, talk, or play together), you will reinforce positive interactions. However, if you give negative attention to your spouse (nagging, fighting, and cutting comments), you will reinforce negative interactions. The behavior or interactions that you attend to will begin to be repeated more and more often.

This may not seem logical when you first look at it. But have you ever found yourself seeming to actually pick a fight with your spouse? Let's look at how that could come about. We know that we want attention and we want to avoid being ignored. Our first choice, of course, would be to get as much positive attention as we can. But let's say our spouse is giving us very little positive attention. As a matter of fact, at times we feel we haven't received any positive attention for days or weeks at a time. We feel completely ignored and unimportant. What can we do? Well, unfortunately even negative attention feels better in most cases than being ignored (at least it's attention). We may find ourselves picking a fight or nagging even more. So, the next time you think your spouse is picking a fight, consider whether you have been ignoring him or her recently and respond with some positive attention.

As you consider this example, you begin to understand the power of attention. In order to treasure our spouse, we must give as much positive attention as we can. This will meet a basic need and will strengthen the positive interactions within the marriage.

Attention can be used to reinforce different types of behavior in your spouse. Attending to your spouse's positive behaviors through compliments and statements of appreciation will help him or her have a desire to continue that behavior. As positive behaviors are reinforced the marriage begins to improve. However, attending to your spouse's negative behaviors will do nothing but increase the negative and therefore damage the marriage. Any behavior you let go by unnoticed will most likely soon drop away. This can be an effective tool for those negative behaviors that you would like to see stopped. But be sure not to ignore attempts and successes at making positive changes. If you do, your spouse will likely stop trying. Noticing and encouraging positive behaviors and attempts to change, and ignoring negative traits and slip-ups is one of the most effective ways to treasure your spouse. You need to give positive feedback and say what he or she is doing right. The power of praise is immeasurable.

## *S*

### *Shield your spouse*

Love always protects ...
*1 Corinthians 13:7*

Again, let's consider that prized trophy or treasured car. Would you consider leaving it outside in the open, exposed to the elements of nature, animals, dirty-fingered kids, and inconsiderate neighbors? Probably not. More likely you would shield it from these elements. You might make sure it has a special place in the garage or on an out-of-reach shelf. You would likely cover it with glass and polish it often, or park at the far end of the parking lot to avoid dings in your doors. You would do your best to protect your treasure.

Do your best to shield and protect your spouse from things that may be harmful to him or her. This may mean providing adequate housing and a safe car to drive. It may mean standing up against those who may be cutting your spouse down (even if they are your family). It may mean walking together in a dark parking lot or holding him or her close during a storm. Maybe it means protecting your spouse from negative aspects of yourself (i.e., mean words, irresponsible behaviors) by working hard to overcome those behaviors. As you focus on treating your spouse like the priceless gift that he or she is, many of these negative aspects of yourself will disappear. Yes, you can control these. You probably already do when you are at work, church, or a new acquaintance's house. But it seems the more comfortable we feel with someone, the more we let down these controls. Don't let comfort do away with appropriate control. All of these positive behaviors are protective in nature and will help your spouse feel treasured by you.

## *U*

### *Understand your spouse's needs*

Understanding is a fountain of life to those who have it.
*Proverbs 16:22*

The differences between men and women are innumerable and evident in practically every area of our lives. What usually happens when we try to meet a need for our spouse is that we give what we think we would need in that same situation. But due to our differences, this is often the wrong thing. The Golden Rule of "Do to others as you would have them do to you" (Luke 6:31) should guide us as a general life-concept, not a "law" related to specific behaviors. In general, how do we want our spouse to treat us? We want our spouse to treat us with respect and to meet our needs. This is what we should do for them as well. However, if we take this verse and apply it to the specific way to do these things for our spouse, we will likely often miss the mark. Here's an example of how that might look. I come home from a really bad day at work and start ranting and raving while pacing back and forth in front of the fireplace. Jim comes into the room (yes, I was talking to myself before he came in), and being the observant and sensitive man he is, he realizes I am very frustrated and now he has to decide what to do. If he applies the Golden Rule specifically he might think to himself, "Well, if I'd had that kind of day I would want Debbie to sit down and listen to me get it off my chest." But if he sits on the loveseat and expectes to attentively listen to me vent,  he would most likely hear me say, "What are you doing? Can't you see I need a hug?"

Or we can reverse the roles. Jim comes home from a really rotten day at the office and is ranting and raving and pacing in front of the fireplace when I walk in. I, being the ever-observant psychologist that I am (although it doesn't take an "Einstein" to assess the situation), quickly assess the situation and realize he is very frustrated. I think to myself, "I know what would help me if I felt like that—a hug." So I proceed directly over to him and start hugging him. He quickly responds with, "Can't you just sit down and listen to me?"

Even though both of us had good intentions and really wanted to meet the other's need to be heard and emotionally supported, we did not help by doing specifically what we would need in that situation. What we should have done instead, is learn what our spouse needed from us and do that. So the "Golden Rule" to apply to behaviors in marriages goes more like this:

The Golden Rule for Marriage: Do unto others as they need you to do.

If we don't take time to find out specifically what our spouse needs, we are likely to not meet that need. Be sure to share openly with your spouse what you need in different situations. Don't expect your spouse to read your mind.

One wife I met with was frustrated that her husband was not meeting her needs. She described wanting him to write her notes or send her cards that expressed how he felt about her. Even as she said this to me, her husband looked shocked. He said, "I never knew you wanted me to do that. You never told me." To which she responded, "Well maybe not with words, but why do you think I keep writing those notes and leaving them in your lunch box or car? I kept hoping you would realize you should do that for me. But you never did."

This wife was holding on to the belief that says, "If I do this for him, he will know I need it, and he'll do it for me." Of course this won't work. I'm sure her husband enjoyed receiving the cards and notes, but because this was not a need for him, he placed less weight on its importance. Two important things happened here that, if left unnoticed, could cause damage in the relationship. First of all, the husband did not pick up on his wife's hint to send her notes and therefore he did not respond by meeting her needs. Because she did not openly state them, her needs went unmet and hurts developed. Second, although the wife was making some very nice gestures toward the husband by sending the notes, she was also not meeting his needs. Doing nice things for your spouse that don't meet his or her needs is like taking your car to get gas and holding the nozzle three feet away. You are expending energy (and money) as you let the gas pour out all over the pavement, and you only get a few drops in the car every now and then. When you give and give in ways that don't meet a need for your spouse, both of you end up feeling empty. Your spouse feels empty because he or she never got refueled. And you feel empty because you don't have an endless supply of energy to give. If you each take the time to genuinely understand what your spouse needs, your efforts to refuel by meeting needs will be much more successful. And as you keep your spouse fueled up, he or she in turn will have the energy to give to you and therefore meet some of the specific needs you have. This is the give-and-take of a healthy relationship.

*Romance*

My lover is mine and I am his.
*Song of Solomon 2:16*

Remember when you were dating and romance seemed to be everywhere? Whatever happened to that? For most couples romance takes a nose dive shortly after marriage. The focus moves away from wining and dining to eating and sleeping. We are confident that we have "caught" him or her and proven to him or her that we care. Then we slack off. How is our spouse to take that feeling of being treasured from dating into marriage if we don't continue the behavior that made him or her feel that way? And even if you weren't a "Casanova" during dating, why not learn to be one now? Treasuring your spouse includes being romantic.

Romance involves proving you think about your spouse when you are not together and showing it when you are together. It involves taking time out of busy schedules to make each other feel loved, cared about, important, and special. It means taking the ordinary (dinner or a walk) and making it extraordinary (candlelit dinner or a walk in the moonlight). Through romantic gestures you tell your spouse that he or she is the one and only one for you and worth the extra effort.

Never forget the importance of dating your spouse. This may seem elementary, but you might be surprised (or maybe not) how many couples don't date anymore. Or, if they do, it is only once or twice a year for special occasions. If you want your relationship to thrive and your spouse to feel treasured, you must spend quality couple time together. If possible, set aside a date night once a week. I have talked to many newlyweds who don't understand the importance of having a date night. They have recently been "dating" and couldn't wait to get married so they could be together all the time. They often expect marriage to be one long date. But it isn't long before they realize how treasured these special times together become.

For some, the once a week date night may be difficult. But remember, you show that you treasure something by acting like it's important to you. Spending time with your spouse shows that he or she is important to you. You may need to change how you have defined "date" due to finances or time constraints. Don't get stuck in the rut of "dinner and a movie." Get creative. Regardless of money and time excuses, you should never go more than one month without having a date. As you get more creative, you may find yourselves having dates every few nights when you realize you don't even have to leave your house or spend any money. The end of this chapter has a list of date suggestions to help you start getting creative.

*Edify your spouse*

Therefore encourage one another and build each other up ...
*1 Thessalonians 5:11*

To edify your spouse means to build him or her up. You treasure your spouse through accepting him or her "as is," good and bad, not focusing on how you want to change him or her. You can help him or her to build up the positive qualities they possess by the way you interact.

You also edify by showing your appreciation for all your spouse does for you. So often the things our spouse does for us on a daily basis go unnoticed or unappreciated. The kindnesses we receive, both large and small, if noticed at all, are often viewed as part of our spouse's job description. Even if we expect certain things, we should never forget to show appreciation for all our spouse does for us. Take time every day to tell your spouse how much you appreciate him or her. It's always nice to hear what someone else likes about us. It reinforces a healthy self-esteem.

## One Final Note

One of the main things I want to emphasize here and throughout this book is that having a strong, healthy, growing marriage does not necessarily take a lot of hard work, but it does take attention. A marriage is like a garden. You spend time preparing for it and cultivating it. Then it begins to grow. What you do next determines the health of the crop. You can sit back and watch it grow—and it will, weeds and all, at least for a while. But without daily attention, it will become overrun with weeds and wither from lack of water and nourishment. Or, you can give the marriage garden a little attention every day, discarding the weeds while they are small and insignificant, and giving life-saving nourishment. If you choose this option, the harvest of your marriage will be overflowing. Beware, the longer you go without giving the daily attention, the more work you will have to put into your garden to get it healthy again. But once that initial work is done, you can easily maintain a healthy garden and marriage through daily attention.

## Application

It's time to learn how to put the principles of treasuring to work in your life and in your marriage. The exercises in this section will help you improve your marriage by learning how better to treasure your spouse.

1. *"You are my sunshine" list.* This exercise is an expansion of your personal "sunshine list" from the previous chapter. The original exercise was developed to help you build your own self-esteem; this one will help you enhance your spouse's self-esteem. Remember, you have a different vantage point when looking at your spouse and therefore are capable of reflecting the "sun" (those positive traits) back to him or her. In this exercise, you will make a list of the positive traits you see in your spouse. List all those things you really like about him or her. You may even want to put it in the form of a love letter. This is like creating a hard copy of your knee-to-knee warm fuzzy exercise from chapter 2.

This exercise serves two purposes. First, it will cause you to keep your thoughts about your spouse positive. Second, when you share it with you spouse, you will be engaging in a behavior that "in love" couples engage in (telling each other what you like about the other), and this makes him or her feel great. They will have a list of all the things you like about them to read as often as they choose.

*2. Wish list.* This is an exercise that developed from something my mom taught me. Mom always had us kids make a wish list at Christmas and birthdays. I think this started as soon as we were able to look at the Sears Wish Book and point to what we liked. She said she never wanted to see a disappointed look on our faces when we opened our gifts. So we made lists of things we wanted, everything from the $2 item to the $200 item (which was huge back then). We loved dreaming and wishing and making the lists. We never knew which things we would get, and we definitely knew we wouldn't get everything on the list. But we did know that everything we got would be something we wanted, something from the list. And Mom never had to worry about disappointed faces. It was like handing her a perfect instructional manual for making us happy on Christmas morning.

I thought about this one day and decided, "Wouldn't it be nice if, when we gave something to our spouse, we knew it was the right thing?" So I adapted Mom's wish list idea to use in marriages.

In this exercise, you are going to create for your spouse the instructional manual for making you feel loved and treasured. You are going to write on paper specific things that your spouse can do to make you feel loved. Wouldn't you like to know exactly the right thing to do or say? I know I sure would. Remember, good instructional manuals are clear and very specific. They give lots of information and detail. So don't get skimpy here. The more you write, the better your spouse will be able to meet your needs.

To start, at the top of a piece of paper write, "I feel loved when you ..." Then fill the paper with things your spouse does or could do that make you feel loved. The list should include things from all of the following categories:

Things he or she used to do but doesn't anymore. My husband and I dated all through high school and we have boxes and boxes of notes we used to write back and forth. I loved getting these notes, but it seemed that after we got married these stopped. One of the things on my list is "I feel loved when you write me love notes." This helped him to start writing me love notes again.

Things he or she does every day. There are things that we do for each other on a daily or weekly basis that become habit or duty. Make sure you identify those things your spouse does on a regular basis that make you feel loved. For example, Jim has always put gas in my vehicle for me. As a matter of fact, I can't remember the last time I did that myself. By putting "I feel loved when you put gas in my car" on my list, I was telling Jim that I appreciate him doing this for me. This also caused a change in his attitude about this activity. He had just seen that as his job or responsibility before. But once he realized it made me feel loved to have him take care of me this way, he had a new perspective on his "job." Examples of this category would be; "I feel loved when you take out the trash," "… clean the house," "… mow the lawn."

Things he or she has never done but you would like. Remember, this is a wish list. As you make your list, think of things that you think you might like to have your spouse do for you. One of the things on my list was "I feel loved when you brush my hair." When Jim read the list he said, "I don't brush your hair." I said, "I know, but I would really like that." Before long he learned that if I came home from a rough day and he had just a few minutes, he could grab the hairbrush, sit behind me, and brush my hair briefly and the bad day seemed to just disappear.

As you write your list, consider the issues of time and money. You should be sure to include things on your list that take practically no time at all to give (e.g., "I feel loved when you wink at me from across the room," "… tell me that you love me," "… rub my back or feet," "… bring me a cup of coffee") all the way up to things that take lots of time (e.g., "I feel loved when you fix me a four-course meal," "… spend your day off planting flowers with me," "… take me away for a long weekend"). Be sure to include things that cost nothing or very little (e.g., "I feel loved when you kiss me before you leave for work," "… send me a card in the mail," "… bring me a single rose") all the way up to things that could cost a fortune (remember it's a wish list and you won't necessarily get everything on the list; e.g. "I feel loved when you take me on a 10-day cruise," "… buy me a sailboat," "… take me on a vacation every year" "… surprise me with a bright red Lexus").

It is very important that you be as specific as possible on this list. Remember the Christmas wish list? It would not have worked to write down "I want a Barbie" on the list. How likely would it have been that Mom would pick out exactly which Barbie I wanted? I had to write, "I want the Barbie with the long red dress and her hair pulled up on top of her head." Now Mom could get just the right one. The same applies to your list. Give enough details and specifics that your spouse will be sure to get it right. Don't say, "I feel loved when you bring me flowers." You might get roses, daisies, wild flowers—dandelions. Be sure to say exactly what you want. If my list said "I feel loved when you bring me a candy bar from the grocery store," and he comes home with an Almond Joy, he would definitely see my disappointed face. However, if he brought me a Butterfinger, I would be his forever. So don't leave room for guesswork. Tell him or her exactly what you would like.

Once each of you have finished your list, exchange them. Be sure to go over everything on the list to be sure you completely understand what each item entails. Then begin doing at least one thing a week off the list for your spouse. (Often, you may be able to do several things on the list each week.)

*3. Have a date.* Once you get back to scheduling regular date nights, you will find yourselves looking forward to these special times. Take turns planning the date from start to finish. When it's his turn, he arranges the babysitter (from a list of approved names from her), chooses the activity, and tells her what type of clothing to wear and when to be ready—nothing more. When it's her turn, she plans it all and even does the driving. He won't know where he's going until he gets there. This will definitely alleviate the problem of, "What do you want to do?" "I don't know. What do you want to do?"

Money may be an excuse you're using not to date. This is not an excuse. If you noticed, I said, "have a date" not "go on a date." In other words, you can learn to date without ever leaving your house. Or, if you decide to leave the house, you can learn to date without spending any (or very little) money. I worked with one couple who definitely was struggling financially. They became very creative with their dating, and actually developed a playful competition. They took turns planning the dates and tried to find out who could come up with the most enjoyable date for the least amount of money. I have included a list of possible dates for all different sized pocketbooks at the end of this chapter. Feel free to use this to help you brainstorm dates that will work for you.

*4. Let's have some fun.* It is important for the two of you to have fun together. What do you do for "play time"? Do you spend your recreational time together or doing your own thing. There is nothing wrong with having some activities that you do separately; however, there is something wrong with doing nothing fun together. You need to develop a list of activities that both of you would enjoy doing together. To do this, each of you should first make your own list of things you enjoy doing for recreation (or things you would be willing to try). Once this is completed, sit down (knee-to-knee) and go over the lists. Then develop a final list of the things both of you have agreed to try together. As you begin engaging in these activities, make a commitment to try any new activity at least two times. If, after two times, one or both of you decides you don't really enjoy that activity, remove it from your list. Be creative with your ideas. The more options you have available for recreation, the more you will do together.

## 50 Date Ideas

1. Watch a sunset or sunrise together.
2. Go window shopping and dream.
3. Pick up some brochures at a travel agent and spend the evening planning a "someday" trip.
4. Have an evening of dinner and slow dancing in your living room.
5. Put on some of your favorite music and work a jigsaw puzzle together.
6. Read the same book then have a discussion group of two.
7. Sit by the fire and read love poems to each other.
8. Check out a two-person play at the library and read it together.
9. Rent or check out a movie and pop popcorn.
10. Have a wrestling match or pillow fight.
11. Play a board game. Keep a running tally.
12. Have an indoor picnic.
13. Go camping in your back yard.
14. Go kite flying.
15. Take a walk hand-in-hand.
16. Have breakfast in bed and read the comics to each other.
17. Give each other a massage. (Don't forget the oils and candles.)
18. Go to the top of a large building and admire the city lights.
19. Test drive a sports car.
20. Browse at an art gallery.
21. Go to a furniture store and "furnish" your dream home.
22. Build a fire, roast marshmallows, and make s'mores.
23. Build a snowman or sandcastle together.
24. Go to a park and play on the playground equipment.
25. Wash the car together. Have fun spraying each other.
26. Go fishing.
27. Participate in a run or walk-a-thon for your favorite charity.
28. Go to the mall. Pretend to have a million dollars and try to spend it all. (Take a calculator.)

29. Have an evening of bowling and junk food.
30. Go to an amusement park.
31. Go horseback riding.
32. Go to an arcade.
33. Recreate your first date or when you proposed.
34. Take a trip to the zoo.
35. Rent a bicycle built for two.
36. Go canoeing or rafting.
37. Go to a carnival or circus.
38. Take a hike in a nature preserve with a picnic lunch.
39. Lie in the sun and watch the clouds. Tell each other what you see.
40. Play a game of putt-putt golf.
41. Go to a local high school, college, or professional sporting event.
42. Rent your dream car and take it on a picnic.
43. Ride in a horse-drawn carriage after dinner.
44. Go to the symphony or theater.
45. Spend the night at a local bed and breakfast.
46. Rent a houseboat or pontoon for the day.
47. Take a class together (massage therapy, cooking, dancing).
48. Go on a hot air balloon ride.
49. Visit or recreate a place that was special to both of you before marriage.
50. Rent a motel room; swim at the pool.

# *50 Romantic Suggestions*

1. Take a walk in the park.
2. Swing on a swing set.
3. Pull out old love letters and read them to each other.
4. Sit by the fire.
5. Give a single rose.
6. Leave a chocolate kiss on his or her pillow.
7. Send or pick flowers "just because."
8. Look at your wedding pictures or video and reminisce.
9. Repeat your wedding vows.
10. Request "your song" on the radio and listen and dance together.
11. Take a candlelight bubble bath together.
12. Kiss her hand.
13. Kiss for one full minute.
14. Slow dance in your living room.

15. Send a note or card through the mail to her at home or work.
16. Leave an "I miss you" message in his suitcase when he leaves for a trip.
17. Make a personal coupon book for your spouse to redeem (back rub, candlelit dinner etc.).
18. Fill the bedroom with candles.
19. Put glow-in-the-dark stars on your bedroom ceiling.
20. Surprise him or her by meeting for lunch.
21. Go parking.
22. Lie on a blanket and watch for shooting stars. Make a wish together!
23. Open the door for her.
24. Leave "I love you" notes all over the house.
25. Play a romantic board game.
26. Play footsies under the table.
27. Hold hands.
28. Fill a box with romantic ideas and have her pick one. Do whatever it says.
29. Celebrate your anniversary *week,* not just the day.
30. Hold her chair for her.
31. Give a hug, and don't let go.
32. Have her serenaded (or do it yourself).
33. Pantomime your feelings for each other.
34. Feed each other chocolate covered strawberries.
35. Build a fire and roast marshmallows.
36. Tell her you love her in front of others.
37. Send him flowers or a basket of goodies.
38. Wear lingerie for him.
39. Leave "invisible" message on bathroom mirror with defogging solution; it will materialize when mirror fogs up.
40. Sit on his lap and snuggle.
41. Order a single banana split with two spoons.
42. Attend a weekend marital retreat.
43. Cook together.
44. Write poems to each other and read them before bed.
45. Make a scrapbook of your life together.
46. Dance in the rain.
47. Send him a virtual card on his computer at work.
48. Make a tape of your favorite love songs and put a personal message at the end.
49. Read Song of Solomon to each other.
50. Listen to your favorite instrumental music by candlelight.

# 5

# Honey, Are You Listening?

## The #1 Principle of Communication

*veryone should be quick to listen,
slow to speak and slow to become angry.*
*James 1:19*

"You just don't understand! You never listen to me anymore!"
Marilyn was crying in my office. Her husband, Jeff, sat beside her
looking confused and frustrated. She had been describing an incident in their home earlier that week that was the last straw for her.

It was Sunday afternoon. Marilyn had wanted to talk to Jeff all
weekend about something at her work that really bothered her. She
had waited because the timing just wasn't right. They had both been
busy all weekend and she wanted Jeff's full attention. So she kept
waiting. She mentioned to him that she wanted to talk when he had
a few minutes. He responded with a grunt and nod from under the
car hood. But he never seemed to have the time. She was beginning
to feel unimportant to him.

Driving home from church Sunday, she looked forward to finding
time to talk. They went through their normal routine of fixing and
eating lunch—well, she did; Jeff checked his e-mail—then getting
their daughter down for her nap. When she came out of the nursery
she planned to bring up the work topic again, thinking it would be a
good time to talk with no interruptions. But, when she walked into

the living room, she found Jeff in his favorite chair watching a golf tournament. She was disappointed and wondered if she should interrupt him. She decided this was important enough and asked Jeff if he had time to talk to her about the work situation. He responded with a "Uh-huh" and a nod of the head but never moved from his spot or turned away from the television.

Marilyn had kept this inside all weekend and was about to burst, so she started spilling her guts even though she knew she didn't have Jeff's full attention. This is better than nothing, she told herself. But she soon realized that maybe it wasn't better than nothing. In the middle of one of her sentences, she heard, "Oh man! I can't believe you missed that putt!" This stopped her cold. She wanted to yell, "You would rather talk to the TV than me!" but she didn't. Instead, she said, "Honey, are you listening?"

Jeff responded with a slight startle and a glance in her direction. "Huh? Oh, yeah. Go on, what were you saying?"

"This is important to me Jeff. I need you to listen to me."

"I am. You were saying something about that customer who was rude to you or something. Right? So, go on. Come on, don't hook it this time."

Marilyn couldn't take it anymore. She walked over to the TV and turned it off.

"Hey, what was that for! He was just about to tee off."

"I'm the one that's 'teed' off! You can't even take a few minutes to listen to me. Everything else is so much more important to you. Well, I can't take it anymore."

You can imagine where it went from there. That's right, straight downhill with lots of anger, defensiveness, accusations, and threats. All of a sudden, as she screamed and got right in his face, Jeff was listening. He was getting the message loud and clear: "If something doesn't change, it's over!"

A few days later, they were in my office, the pain and damage from this incident still evident on their faces. After Marilyn shared what happened that day with me, I asked Jeff what he was thinking about. He remembered the situation much the same way as Marilyn had just told it. "But I just don't understand what the big deal was. Why did she blow up like that? I heard everything she said. At one point I even repeated most of it back to her. But that just seemed to make things worse. I thought that's what she wanted, to know that I heard her. Well, I did! So why are we sitting here rehashing the whole thing? Just because I didn't turn the TV off? I can do more than one thing at a time, you know!"

What was the big deal? After all, Jeff said he heard what she was saying. He even proved that by repeating it back to her. Shouldn't that have been enough? Obviously it wasn't. Marilyn walked away from the conversation feeling discounted. Can something as little as not being heard have that much impact and do that much damage to someone's sense of self-worth? The answer is most definitely yes!

## *The Warm Fuzzy of Being a Good Listener*

I have often heard, "He just doesn't listen to me!" or, "She doesn't understand where I'm coming from," or "I feel totally ignored when I try to talk." All of these indicate that someone has been receiving cold pricklies. The major principles of communication have broken down and the relationship is being damaged. One of the most important warm fuzzies in the treasure box of your marriage is being a good listener to your spouse. The skills of communication are some of the most important keys to any relationship. The way you communicate can increase the warm fuzzy experience and strengthen the bond between the two of you, or it can add to the cold prickly experiences and eventually cause irreparable damage.

What is the most important aspect of communication? What key concept is powerful enough to make or break any relationship simply by its presence or absence?

Listening.

Can it really be that basic? You bet!

Listening is the foundational and most crucial level of communication. Studies have shown that we spend nearly 80 percent of our waking hours communicating and about 45 percent of that is spent listening or hearing.[1] So, if nearly 50 percent of communication time is listening, we'd better be good at this skill. However, most of us are not. Classes all over the country teach how to be a better communicator (what they mean is how to be a better speaker). College students take required courses on writing and speaking. But I have had a difficult time finding a place where we are actively taught to be better listeners.

Another study reported that people actually retain only 65 percent of what is said to them—and only retain it a very few moments.[2] This gap between the spoken word and the perceived word indicates that as a group we definitely are not skilled listeners. The responsibility for communication breaking most likely falls on the shoulders of the listener. An abundance of people are willing to do the talking; but the most valuable person, and likely the person in the most demand, is the one who is willing to listen.

Being a good listener is essential to healthy communication. We must learn to listen first and most, then everything else will begin to fall into place. James 1:19 seems to drive this point home: "Everyone should be quick to listen, slow to speak …"

As I help couples like Marilyn and Jeff examine the earlier stages of their relationship more closely; it becomes evident that both used to be great listeners. Marilyn remembers feeling important to Jeff during the dating and early marriage stage. He took time to listen to the events of her day, even the mundane parts. He seemed interested in what she had to say. She even recalled one Saturday when she came home from work in a grouchy mood. Jeff was relaxing in front of the TV. He seemed fairly involved in what he was watching. After a brief greeting she collapsed on the loveseat, planning to just zone out. Before she knew it, Jeff had turned the TV off and was sitting beside her, rubbing her legs and asking what was wrong. "He always seemed so in tune with what was going on with me. He would listen patiently until I was done talking or venting. I don't know if he even realized how much that helped, just to get it off my chest and to feel he really cared. He didn't have to say a thing, but I knew he understood. Now he either jumps in and tries to fix it for me, or doesn't seem to hear me at all and just goes on talking about whatever he was thinking about. And I've noticed now that if he doesn't say anything at all, I feel ignored. What's happened?"

Although this is a damaging progression in a relationship, it's one that I have seen happen time and time again. One of the strongest warm fuzzies early in a relationship is listening attentively. We begin a relationship, actively showing our partner how important he or she is to us by listening. I can't imagine falling in love with someone who never cared about what I had to say. Most likely all of us spent hours listening to our spouses and making sure they knew we were listening. We were not as concerned about what we had to say as we were in making sure they said what they needed to say. However, over time, our selfish natures seem to take over. We begin to spend less time focused on what the other person is saying, and more time focused on what we want to say. We begin to feel that what we have to say is unimportant to our spouse. Before long, we just stop talking.

"Why waste my time, he doesn't care what I think anyway."

"Why should I tell her how I feel? She always seems to think she knows better than I do."

Statements like these are the kiss of death to open communication.

Have you ever tried to hold a conversation with a brick wall (I mean other than your spouse)? There is no conversation. It's just one person talking (and maybe answering, but that's for another book). Conversation happens when there is an exchange of ideas or feelings. It would seem almost impossible to have an "exchange" with only one person involved in the conversation. Listening is what makes true conversations happen.

There is no communication without listening!

As you will soon learn, saying nothing actually says very much. I see the power of listening every day in my office. My profession is built on the ability to be a good listener. As a matter of fact, I spend many therapeutic hours in silence. These hours often have the most impact on my patients. Clients walk away feeling accepted, understood, and validated. They return with a feeling of trust and willingness to share even more. Trust grows out of the experience of feeling heard and understood, and this draws people closer together.

Note that listening is not a passive activity. It requires full concentration and active involvement. Although the concept of listening is quite simple (e.g., "You mean all I have to do is be quiet and listen to her, and that will really make her feel better? I don't have to do anything?"), the act of listening is not as simple. Listening, when done correctly, does in fact require attention.

## *Listening versus Hearing*

Let's take some time to identify the skills involved in being a good listener. Some of these may seem basic, but they are all essential. Listening means more than not talking, although that is the beginning point. It is important to understand the difference between listening and hearing. The words listening and hearing are often used interchangeably. However, if you examine the definitions, you will see there is a difference.

Hearing is simply perceiving sound. Sound waves hit your ear drums and they vibrate. *Listening*, however, means you are paying active attention to what that sound is. The goal of listening is to reach a deeper understanding of your spouse. "Understanding is a fountain of life to those who have it" (Proverbs 16:22). Proverbs 11:12 says, "A man of understanding holds his tongue." That sounds to me like understanding is not only vital and valuable, but also something that cannot be reached without being quiet and listening (holding our tongue). Norman Wright, in his book, *Communication: Key to Your Marriage,* says, "Listening is more than politely waiting your turn to speak. It is more than hearing words. Real listening is receiving and accepting the message as it is sent—seeking to understand what the other person really means."[3] When you move beyond hearing and into listening, true understanding begins to occur.

Jesus taught about the difference between hearing and listening in the parable of the sower in Matthew 13. As the farmer went out to sow his seed, the seed fell on four different types of soil that produced four different results. The seed that fell on the path was quickly eaten by birds. The seed that fell on the rocky places with shallow soil grew quickly then withered because it had no roots. The seed that fell among the thorns was choked out. And, finally, the seed that fell on the good soil grew and produced a crop.

Jesus explains this parable to his disciples in Matthew 13:18–23. The seed is the gospel of Christ and the soil represents people. The first three soils "hear" the word of God. They are presented with the message, but either ignore it or hear it without fully grasping its meaning. However, the fourth soil really listens to the message. "But the one who received the seed that fell on good soil is the man who hears the word and understands it" (Matthew 13:23).

Now that you know the basic concepts of listening, how do you actually apply these to conversations with your spouse? Putting all the concepts of listening together into one conversation that results in understanding each other is done through a technique I call ECHO Conversation. This process may seem awkward at first and will require some practice.

## *Why Not "Just Do It"?*

I once had a man ask me, "So why all these definitions and homework assignments about listening? What's the big deal? Seems to me if you want to be a better listener you just do it." That would be great if it worked that way, but I've never seen it happen. Learning any new skill takes time and practice. You don't just will it into existence.

When I was learning to play the piano as a little girl, I very much wanted to just sit down and play a song. But simply deciding that I was going to play didn't allow me to produce "Beethoven's Fifth Symphony" the first time I played. I started with something more like "Twinkle, Twinkle, Little Star." Then gradually (and I do mean gradually), and with much blood, sweat, and prodding from my mother along with the constant practice logs, I eventually made it to

"Beethoven's Fifth" (or did I just dream that?). This and every other skill you choose to learn will take effort and practice on your part. ECHO Conversation is no different. With practice it will become more comfortable and natural. You will soon realize how much smoother your conversations go when you employ these skills. You will both feel you have been heard and understood before you end the conversation.

## *ECHO Conversation*

ECHO conversation is a technique that combines all the necessary elements of listening in such a way that your spouse will know for sure that you have understood what he or she was trying to say. ECHOing involves the process of actively focusing your attention on what your spouse is saying, including verbal and nonverbal information, and then reflecting back or "echoing" what you heard. It is based loosely on the natural phenomenon of an echo. Have you ever stood at the entrance of a cave or the bottom of a canyon and bellowed out some word or phrase hoping to hear your words echoed back to you? Children and adults alike seem thrilled to hear their words return to them and will often continue to yell out even ridiculous phrases and wait with anticipation for the echo. But can you imagine the looks on their faces if they yelled out, "I love you," and a moment later the cave echoed "Who cares" or "Yeah, sure you do." Yet, in our marriages, conversations can become that distorted. Using ECHO conversation will help you hear what your spouse is really trying to say.

Let's break ECHOing into its four parts to help you understand how it works in conversation.

**E Establish and Explain**
**C Concentrate**
**H Highlight the Main Points**
**O Obtain Agreement/Understanding**

### *Establish and Explain*

The first step in ECHOing is to establish the topic. Either you or your spouse need to define what the issue is you want to discuss and then pick a time to sit down and talk (e.g., "Honey, I really need to talk to you about our plans for summer vacation. Could we make some time around 8:00 tonight?").

One of you will be identified as the speaker and the other, of course, is the listener. The speaker's job is to explain his or her thoughts and feelings about the established topic. This should be done as concisely as possible. Remember that your spouse is trying to listen and prepare to echo. If you go off on a 10-minute tirade, most of what you say will get lost. Be concise and to the point. (More about how to talk in the next chapter.)

# *C*

### *Concentrate*

As the speaker talks, the listener's job is to listen! This means you must stop talking and concentrate on what the person is saying as well as on how it's being said. Focus your attention on the words and ideas. But be sure not to miss the attitudes and feelings also being expressed through body language, tone of voice, gestures, and facial expressions. These nonverbal aspects of communication often will give you an accurate indication of what the speaker's attitude and emotional state are, regardless of the words being said.

While listening and concentrating, be careful not to interrupt either verbally or mentally. Interrupting is probably the most destructive element to communication. Give the person talking time to say what he or she has to say; any questions you have may be addressed if you are patient. This can be difficult because we want to say what we think when we think it. Even if we are not verbally interrupting we may be mentally interrupting. Mental interruptions include arguing in your head or jumping to conclusions and assuming you know what the person will say next. When you do this, you tune yourself out from the rest of what the speaker has to say and begin to formulate your rebuttal. You are deciding what your comeback is going to be or maybe just arguing within yourself, "I can't believe she just said that!" You may be thinking, "Hurry up and finish; I've got your point" or "Yes, yes, I know what you mean." Not only does this show disrespect for your spouse, but also you just may be wrong in your conclusions. Waiting and listening will keep you from putting your foot in your mouth or from starting an argument. But even more importantly, it shows that you value what your spouse is saying as more important than what you may want to say.

Concentrating also means avoiding outside distractions. The TV, telephone, cooking dinner, or children all fit into this category. It is practically impossible to concentrate on what the speaker is saying with only part of your brain working on it. Really listening requires you to focus your attention. Choosing the right time to hold an important conversation will help tremendously. Don't attempt to hold a conversation of importance right before your spouse's favorite TV program or if you are expecting an important call or fixing dinner. Parents of young children seem to be especially affected in this area. It seems inevitable that our children need to talk to us the minute we attempt to hold an important adult conversation. Many mothers actually become quite good at hearing and even responding to multiple conversations simultaneously. Responding, however, is not listening and should be avoided during important conversations with your spouse. If you choose to talk about serious matters during these times, you are flirting with disaster. Unless it is vitally important and you can can't talk about it at a different time, I would suggest that you avoid times that you know will be packed with distractions.

## H

### *Highlight the Main Points*

Just as in a cave, once the speaker has finished, there is a brief pause and then the echo comes. When your spouse has finished speaking, take just a moment to consider what you have heard, then echo it. However, unlike in the cave, the words reflected back may not be exactly those words spoken. The echo should reflect the main points of what your spouse presented along with any emotional undertones that may have changed the meaning of the words you were hearing. You will be summarizing what you heard by adding in all the cues you were aware of and the main points presented. It is important to remember here that this is not the place or time for you to add in your own personal thoughts, opinions, judgments, or rebuttals. There will be time for that later. Just focus on what the speaker said.

Let's say the speaker is sitting with arms and legs crossed and turned away from you. With an angry scowl in a rough, loud voice he or she says "No! I'm not angry!" You could respond, "What I heard you say is that you are not angry. Is that what you meant to say?" But if that were your response, you would not have been using the ECHO conversation skills. You would just have been hearing. The ECHO response would have been, "What I heard you say is that you are angry, but you don't want to talk about it right now. Is that what you meant to say?" See the difference? ECHOing takes into account all you are seeing, hearing, and sensing in order to come to a conclusion. At times you will sound as though you are repeating exactly what you heard. That's okay. Actually, the more open and honest the speaker is, the less interpretation the listener will have to do, and the more clear the "echo" will be.

As you may have noticed in the example above, there were two phrases used by the listener that were not said by the speaker. These are crucial in ECHOing. The first is, "What I heard you say was …" This should be the first phrase said by the listener. This is different than, "What you said was …" The latter statement implies that the listener will be right. What if the speaker doesn't agree that what was repeated back was an accurate representation of what was said? This can quickly lead to one or both parties becoming defensive and an argument about who said what or who's right will likely begin. A simple change in words can avoid this. "What I heard you say was …" allows room for either party to change or disagree without the issue of who is right or wrong.

The second key phrase, "Is that what you meant to say?" should be the final phrase the listener says. This differs from, "Is that what you said?" If the latter is used, and the speaker says "No, that's not what I said;" then the right and wrong issue comes up again. This time, however, it looks like the listener is the one who is wrong. Regardless of who's right or wrong, defenses rise and the conversation quickly becomes nonproductive. Asking, "Is that what you meant to say?" allows the speaker to hear how he or she came across to the listener and adjust communication without either person becoming defensive.

## *O*

### *Obtain Agreement/Understanding*

The final step in ECHO conversation involves the listener obtaining agreement from the speaker that he or she has completely heard and understood what the speaker was trying to say. This agreement must be reached before giving the listener a turn to discuss the established topic. The speaker says what he or she needs to say, followed by the listener echoing that back. The listener must do this without interjecting his or her own ideas or judgments. The listener is simply listening and will have a turn to address the issue later. Once the listener asks, "Is that what you meant to say?" the speaker replies with "Yes" if the listener did get the main points, or "No" if the listener missed something or if the speaker wants to adjust what he or she was trying to say. This process should continue until the speaker feels he or she has been completely heard. You will know this agreement has been obtained when the speaker responds with "Yes!" to, "Is that what you meant to say?"

## Both Have a Chance to Speak

ECHO conversation may end at this point. Some conversations involve only one spouse needing to share a thought or feeling about something personal. In those cases, the ECHOing is complete when that speaker feels completely heard and understood. However, many marital conversations involve both of you needing the chance to express yourself and be understood. When this is the case, simply take turns being speaker and listener. The first speaker stays in that role until all four steps of ECHOing are completed. Then the second speaker should address the original issue as if he or she had been the first one to speak. Share original thoughts and feelings about the topic, instead of responding to what the other person just said. There will be time for that later.

## It Really Does Work

Let me share with you how one couple used these skills while discussing their plans for the holiday season.

Jackie and Rob had lived in a small southern Missouri town for about five of their six years of marriage. It seemed that every holiday season brought on additional stress for them, especially about making the trip back home to see their parents. Both sets of parents lived two states away, approximately 45 minutes from each other. Their holiday visits were focused on traveling between their two families and making sure that everyone got the same amount of their time (to be fair). The last three years were even more stressful since they were traveling with two young children. But, they had to go, didn't they? The grandparents, after all, didn't get to see the kids very often, and it's Christmas.

After learning the skills of ECHOing, they were ready to practice. They chose this topic to begin since the holidays were quickly approaching. Jackie agreed to act as the first speaker and took a few minutes to sort out her thoughts and feelings.

Jackie: "I have been thinking about what I would like to do this year over Christmas ever since last year. Although I do enjoy visiting our families and spending part of the holidays with them, I don't like all the pressure I feel to keep things fair between our families. I feel like I have missed the real meaning of Christmas. And, besides, you and I always seem to end up fighting. I'm not sure this is what I want Christmas to be for us and our kids. I also know you like to go to see your family as much as I like to see mine. Well, anyway, I was thinking that I would really like to stay home this year for Christmas. We could focus on setting our own family traditions and be more relaxed. Then maybe we could go to Texas the next week around New Year's and celebrate with them then. That's all."

Rob: "What I heard you say was that you know that we both like to visit with our families, especially around the holidays. But, that for the last few years, you have not enjoyed Christmas the way you want to because of all the pressure to be fair with our time and because of the fighting you and I end up doing. And that what you want to do instead is stay home this year, start our own traditions and then go see our families over New Year's. Is that what you meant to say?"

Jackie: "Yeah, mainly. But I'm not saying that's what we have to do. If you still want to go, maybe we could work something out to have some time here and some time there."

Rob: "Okay, what I heard you say is that what you would like to do is to stay home for Christmas, but that you are worried that maybe that's not what I want to do. And, if I don't want to do that, then you are willing to look at other options. Is that what you meant to say?"

Jackie: "Yes, that's what I was trying to say."

I told them how well they had done so far. I then reminded Rob that it was his turn to share what he would like to do for the holidays as if he had been the first speaker. He took a minute to consider what he wanted to say, then began.

Rob: "Anymore, it seems to me that when I think about Christmas coming up, I just don't get excited the way I used to. I think more about the negatives like the eight-hour drive to your mom and dad's, the kids fussing all the way, the worrying about who might be getting their feelings hurt, and on and on. The positives just seem so far outweighed. I have seriously considered not going to Texas at all around Christmas, too. I think we could have a wonderful Christmas right here at home. I'm done."

Jackie: "What I heard you say is that you have been frustrated with how we have been spending Christmas. And that you feel much more focused on the negatives around our trip home such as the long drive with the kids fussing and worrying about parents getting their feelings hurt than you are about the positives. I also heard you say that you have seriously considered staying here for Christmas and actually think we could make that a wonderful time together. Is that what you meant to say?"

Rob: "Yeah, you got it."

I again praised them for a job well done. I told them at this point they could move to the more natural back-and-forth flow of a conversation and return to ECHOing as needed.

Jackie: "Wow, I can't believe you said that! I was so nervous bringing up the idea because I thought you wouldn't like it. I thought the most important thing about Christmas to you was to be with family, no matter how stressful that might be. I had wanted to ask about this last year, but I was sure you would disagree."

Rob: "I do think the most important part is being with family. But I guess I'm realizing that the four of us are family and you are the ones I want to be with and make Christmas great for. And, believe it or not, I thought you wouldn't like the idea for the same reasons you were thinking I wouldn't like it. Boy, I can't believe we never talked about this before. I just assumed I knew what you were thinking. Guess we were both wrong. You do realize that if we don't go to Texas your mom will give you a big guilt trip. Are you ready for that?"

Jackie: "I think so. Especially now that I know we both want this. I know it won't be easy, but I think it will be worth it."

Both were smiling not only because of their decision, but even more so when they realized that the mind reading they had been doing didn't get either one of them what they wanted. Now they had a new skill that would allow them to check things out and really communicate.

I asked them to take one more step: to summarize what they are hearing the final decision to be. This will help make sure there were no miscommunications.

Rob: "Okay. What I have heard us saying is that we both really want to stay home for Christmas this year and start our own family traditions. We want to be more relaxed and more focused on the real meaning of Christmas. I also heard us say that we would like to see the families, but just not right on Christmas day. I think your idea of going down over New Year's is great. Is that what you have heard us saying?"

Jackie: "Yeah, that's what I heard too. You know what? I am really looking forward to Christmas this year. It's going to be great!"

Rob: "Me, too!"

Rob and Jackie left my office that day hand in hand and chatting about baking sugar cookies to decorate. When they returned after the holidays, they reported having the best Christmas ever. They did see their families over New Year's and had a belated Christmas celebration with them. Everyone actually seemed to enjoy the extension of the season. Rob and Jackie had learned that taking time to listen to each other actually drew them closer together and helped each get needs met that the other had not known about.

## Application

1. *Identify Your Weaknesses.* As you work on becoming a better listener, the first step is to identify what areas of listening you have the most difficulty with so you can focus on those. To help you do this I have listed out the main concepts of ECHOing and included them at the end of this chapter for easy photocopying. Each of you should go through the list and mark those steps that you know are difficult for you personally. Then sit together and discuss the lists. It will be very important at this point that you each ask for constructive feedback about your listening skills. If you don't, you will probably get it anyway; and it is much easier to hear if you asked for it.

For example, if you show your spouse your list and the areas of weakness you identified in yourself, he or she will most likely make some comments whether or not you ask for them. If you don't ask, what you are most likely to hear is: "You didn't mark interrupting? I can't believe it! You are terrible about interrupting. You should have marked that one." By then, you are probably interrupting with some defensive comment and the conversation will go downhill from there. If you openly ask for feedback, it can go much more smoothly. If, as you share your list with your spouse, you say, "These are the areas I know I have trouble with. Are there any others that you have noticed I need to work on too?" Then, when your spouse lovingly responds, "I think you have trouble with interrupting, too," it isn't nearly as hard to accept. Remember that your spouse may have a better idea of your areas of weakness than you do. After all, he or she has been the one on the other side of these conversations. Take feedback seriously.

2. *ECHO Conversation Exercise.* As you begin practicing these skills, do so with a light, non-emotional topic. Remember, you never sit down at a piano for the first time and attempt to play "Beethoven's Fifth Symphony." You start with something more like "Twinkle, Twinkle, Little Star." The same should apply to learning to listen. If you start with something easy, then you can focus on the technique and not on the emotions. As you get better and more comfortable with the skill, then move up to slightly more difficult topics. You'll find several possible starting topics at the end of this section.

Once you have chosen a topic, review the rules and key phrases, and choose who will begin. You should use the knee-to-knee position described in the application section of chapter 2 when doing this exercise. The speaker establishes the topic, takes a few minutes to think about what he or she wants to say and then explains it briefly. The listener should concentrate and actively attend to the speaker by making eye contact, nodding and so on to show he or she is paying attention. Once the speaker finishes, the listener should echo back what he or she heard, using the key phrases "What I heard you say was …" and "Is that what you meant to say?" Remember, do this without adding any of your own ideas, reactions, or emotions.

For example, if the speaker says "I feel we should go to San Francisco for vacation this summer," don't respond with: "What I heard you say was that you think we should go to San Francisco for vacation this summer. But you know we can't afford that kind of trip this year. We just bought a new house and need to stay home and save money." You will have a chance to say your thoughts later.

Your job as listener is just to listen!

Once the listener has obtained agreement that the speaker has felt heard and understood, then switch roles and the new speaker repeats the steps as if he or she were the first one to talk on the topic. Once both of you have felt heard, then you can begin to respond to each other's ideas and comments and move toward a solution. There may be a more natural back-and-forth flow of the conversation at this stage. You should return, however, to the ECHOing, including the key phrases, at any point in the conversation where either one of you does not feel completely heard or if you are not sure you understood what your spouse meant. You can do this by simply saying, "Could you repeat what you heard me say, please?" or, "I would like to repeat what I just heard." As you practice this and move past the awkward use stage, you will likely find yourselves using it on a regular basis.

Set scheduled practice times about two or three times a week at first. These should be times where you will be uninterrupted for at least 15 minutes. The TV should be off, phone unplugged, and kids in bed for you to feel fairly sure this time has been set aside for just the two of you.

## *Suggestions for Starter Topics*

Where we should go on vacation.
How or where we plan to spend the holidays.
How we would like to spend our tax return money.
Division of family chores.
Setting family rules.

## *Parts of ECHO Conversation*

**E: Establish & Explain**

Establish the topic to be discussed.
Explain concisely your thoughts and feelings to the listener.

**C: Concentrate**

Stop talking. You can't effectively listen while you are talking.
Concentrate your attention on the speaker. This includes making eye contact, open body posture, nodding your head, etc. to let the speaker know you are listening.
Concentrate on what the person is saying. Focus your attention on the words, the ideas, and the feelings being related.
Listen to how something is said. Notice the speaker's body language, tone of voice, gestures, and facial expressions.
Don't interrupt verbally.
Don't argue mentally.

Don't jump to conclusions. Avoid tuning out a speaker when you think you have the gist of what he/she is saying or going to say next. When you do this, you tune yourself out from the rest of what the speaker has to say.

Avoid distractions. This includes TV, telephone, children, etc. You may be able to hear more than one thing at a time, but you cannot effectively listen to more than one conversation at a time.

### H: Highlight the Main Points

Pause briefly. To consider what you have heard before giving ECHO response.

Summarize. Present the main ideas along with emotional undertones.

Use the two key phrases. "What I heard you say was ..." and "Is that what you meant to say?"

### O: Obtain Agreement/Understanding

Continue the above steps until the speaker says "yes" to being understood.

# *"Let's Talk"*

The #2 Principle of Good Communication

*D*o not let any unwholesome talk come out of your mouths, but only what is helpful for building others up according to their needs, that it may benefit those who listen."
*Ephesians 4:29*

One late afternoon in January several years ago a very upset woman called my office. Her name was Brittany, and she was crying uncontrollably. My secretary struggled to understand her and gather the necessary information about what was wrong. With a gasping and shaking voice Brittany tried to convey her need to see a counselor "right away, I can't take this anymore!" She described the problem in her own words like this: "My husband hates me! He never talks to me anymore; he won't even fight with me. I feel like we are constantly in a war—a cold war! He can go for days without saying more than a couple of words to me. I'm tired of being ignored!" We scheduled an appointment later that week for both Brittany and her husband, Todd.

When Brittany entered my office she was alone, disheveled and unkempt—not at all what I had expected, knowing that she worked in banking. Her eyes were red and puffy from crying. She wore sweats and an old tattered sweatshirt. Her hair was pulled back into a ragged ponytail. What makeup she did have on was tear-streaked and smudged. As she sat on the sofa, she immediately began to cry.

She apologized and said, "This seems to be all I do lately, cry, cry, cry. I can't seem to stop. I feel like my life is falling apart. What's wrong with me? Why won't my husband talk to me? When I told him I had made a counseling appointment, he looked shocked and said 'Why?' How can he not realize there's a problem here? We never talk anymore, not even about little things. I used to feel so close to him. I could tell him anything. But now he never seems interested in anything I have to say. He never asks how my day was or what I think about what's happening in the Middle East. Nothing! We used to talk about everything. Lately I've found myself trying to pick a fight with him just to get him to say something. I hate that!" I helped Brittany calm down and she started telling me about her relationship with Todd.

They dated for two years before they married. They were each in their mid-thirties, and neither had been married before. They had been more focused on developing their careers and enjoying time with friends. A mutual friend introduced them, sure they would be just perfect for each other. They hit it off immediately. From the beginning they seemed to have much in common and they could talk about anything. They went on several "traditional" dates of dinner and a movie, but they soon realized that what they enjoyed most were their long discussions.

Brittany remembered these debates from early in their relationship. "We used to be able to talk about anything, no matter how touchy the subject was. We would spend hours on the phone or at a park discussing everything from our future together to religion to politics. Believe it or not, the topics that we didn't agree on seemed to be the most fun to discuss. We actually seemed to like hearing each other's point of view. We didn't have to agree. Now we don't even get far enough into the conversation to find out if we agree or not. Instead, Todd just shuts up and we end up not talking at all. I feel so unimportant to him. The reason our friend set us up together in the first place was because she always heard Todd say he would like a girl with a good head on her shoulders, who could think for herself and say what she was thinking. That was me. And Todd always said how much he liked hearing my point of view. Well, at least early on that's what he said. Now I think he just wants me to be seen and not heard."

I hear this over and over. I have worked with couples from a variety of ages and lengths of marriage. They have come from different backgrounds and cultures and the entire range of income and social status. They all had one major thing in common: an inability to communicate. "We just can't talk to each other anymore!"

As I meet with these couples, I soon see that they usually can remember times early in their relationship when conversation was effortless. They talked for hours on end about practically nothing and everything all at the same time. Like Todd and Brittany, many couples remember long, late night talks that drew them close together. Many couples say that one of the reasons they decided to get married was because they could communicate so well. They knew that they could handle just about anything if they could just talk it through, and they felt they could talk about anything.

So what happened? Why, now, do they seem to choose to sit in silence for hours on end? Or even worse, why do they fight and argue more often than they share thoughts and feelings? Somewhere along the way, they stopped talking things through, and before they knew it, the relationship began to fall apart. Eventually, couples get to the point that they seem only to be able to talk about surface things or daily routine issues such as "Who's going to pick the kids up after work?" or "What should we have for dinner?" And sometimes even those topics aren't discussed very well.

What happened to that couple who seemed to have such good communication skills early on? Did they somehow lose those skills that allowed them to have endless conversations? No, of course not. As a matter of fact, I usually witness firsthand that they still have the skills available to them because they use these skills in their interactions with me. They are also most likely using these same skills in other areas of life such as work, church, with friends and children. So why not in their most important relationship?

You may be asking yourself, "Is talking really so important that a marriage could truly fall apart without it?" Let's look at what talking brings to a relationship and therefore, what would be missing without it. Then you can decide just how high it should be on the priority list of warm fuzzies.

## *Why Is Talking So Important?*

Talking is one of the strongest ways to build intimacy and closeness, and therefore one of the most important aspects of any relationship, especially marriage. One reason we tend to communicate "better" and "more" during the dating stage of a relationship is because it is then that we are focused on building intimacy and closeness. Once we feel the relationship is established, we tend to stop focusing on building it and too often believe it to be a "finished project" in need of little or no attention in the future. Unlike building a "maintenance-free" home, a relationship is never a "finished project." For the home, there is a definite time where the building stops and the project is considered "complete." However, a relationship will require constant attention and maintenance to stay healthy.

Building good communication skills, which includes striking a balance between talking and listening, will be one of the most beneficial ways to improve your relationship. Can you imagine a relationship where both people only talked or both only listened? That could be miserable. Both of you need to be able to talk and listen effectively. You can't have one without the other, and one is not any more important than the other.

Do you believe that just talking (regardless of what you may be talking about) could build a stronger and more intimate marriage? Can talking about who won the playoff game last night or what the weather is supposed to be next week or about the great deal you got at the sidewalk sale today really bring those benefits? Not likely.

In the last chapter we learned that just sitting quietly and "hearing" is not what builds intimacy. Building intimacy requires listening. Just talking, regardless of the topic, will not grow intimacy. The treasure of intimacy is only reached when we dig deep into ourselves and share from our hearts.

Let's say you are on a quest for buried treasure. You have the map and have carefully followed all the directions and have moved past each landmark in the correct order. Now, you have reached the place where "X" marks the spot. You start looking around for your treasure and it's nowhere to be seen. Did you take a wrong turn somewhere? Miss a landmark? You look at the map again and are sure you are in the right place. So now what? Were you really expecting it to just be sitting right there out in the open? Of course not. And then it dawns on you—it's time to dig. As you wonder how deep you will have to go, you realize the more valuable the treasure, the deeper you have to dig. How deep are you willing to dig for the treasure of intimacy?

## Digging Deeper for Intimacy

People communicate at any one of five different levels as they go through their day and interact with those around them. If talking about just anything developed intimacy, then we would likely all go around feeling very intimate with our coworkers, grocery clerks, mail delivery persons, and bill collectors. We know this is not the case. So let's take time to understand these different levels and determine at what level the benefits of closeness and intimacy develop.

Every day we talk and communicate with those around us. As a matter of fact, the world and each of our individual lives would not continue as we know it if it were not for people everywhere communicating in one way or another. Of course, some of the actual means of communication have changed and diversified drastically over the years. We have moved from chiseling words into stone, to handwriting on paper, to me sitting here at my computer, and, for the truly advanced and up-to-date, to speaking the words into written form. We have moved from stagecoach express to Federal Express and then onto e-mail and instant messages. Then there is my personal favorite, a means of communication that has never changed and hopefully never will—talking, that wonderful old stand-by of chatting face-to-face with a good friend over a cup of coffee (or soda, if you're more like me and haven't grown up enough to drink the hard stuff).

Regardless of the means of communication, the levels at which we communicate and share of ourselves with the world around us have not changed. Depending on the relationship you have with the person you are talking to, you may share at any one of five levels of communication as defined by John Powell in his book, *Why Am I Afraid to Tell You Who I Am?*[1] The following explanation of these levels is loosely adapted from his definitions.

*Scratching the Surface: Level 1.* You've reached the place where "X" marks the spot and are ready for your treasure. You scan the terrain visually and maybe kick at the sand a bit to move it around and see if anything is directly under the surface. Of course there is not, because the treasure of intimacy is not at this level. So you take some time to rest and catch your breath. We don't have anything of ourselves to give at this stage. In communication, this level is the "safest" but also the most distant and detached level of communication. It is superficial and involves no personal sharing. At this level we often ask questions that either we don't really care if we get an answer to, don't care what the answer is, or already know what the answer is "supposed" to be. For example, "How are you?" "Where did you get that hat?" or maybe "Did you enjoy the movie?" These interactions are brief and often viewed only as a social obligation, not as a desire to really get to know the other person.

*Hands in the Sand: Level 2.* Rested and more ready to interact, we fall to our knees and begin to dig in the sand with our hands. We know we won't be able to dig very deep this way, but it's a good starting point.

Conversation at this level involves playing news reporter and talking about others and what they may have said or done. We merely report the facts, much like the six o'clock news. We don't expand on or enhance the facts by presenting our personal opinion or feelings related to the information. It's always safer and easier to talk about others than to open up and share about ourselves. This level is slightly deeper than the first in that the information shared is something we feel will be of interest to someone. However, we take no personal risk because the information is not about us. Examples include comments like: "Did you hear about Bob and Mary? They're having some marital problems." or "There was an accident on the Expressway that had traffic backed up for five miles."

*Grabbing the Shovel: Level 3.* You've gone as deep as you can without breaking out the tools, but now you are ready to start getting serious about this treasure thing. You are grabbing the tools and putting yourself into the task at hand, but still only with minor risks. You may jump into the area where you are digging, but only if you could just as easily jump right back out.

This is the first level of real communication. At this level we begin to take risks. We may present information from the previous level and then add in our own personal thoughts and ideas about that information. We also may simply present our opinions, judgments and decisions on their own. Either way, at this level we share cautiously and will retreat quickly if we feel that what we are saying is not being accepted. This is the "I think ..." level, where we share what's in our minds. We may debate our positions, but only from a logical point of view, continuing to keep our feelings far from view. Examples of this level of conversations would include: "I think all restaurants should be smoke-free," or "I'm considering getting a part-time job to help out with the finances."

*In Neck Deep: Level 4.* You can't dig any deeper unless you are willing to jump down in that hole that you know is just about as deep as you are tall, and it will only continue to get deeper. Quick escape will no longer be an option, and you will begin to feel vulnerable as you realize you will need someone to help you out. Is the treasure really worth it to you? Do you trust your companion to stay close by and help as needed? You decide yes and jump in.

At this level, we have reached the point of true risk taking. This is the "I feel ..." level where we open up and share from our hearts and express our feelings and emotions. We may still present information from the earlier levels of facts and our ideas or judgments about those facts, but we go one step deeper and also share the feelings underneath the thoughts. If true intimacy is going to develop between two people, they must both reach the point of opening up and sharing from their feelings. Examples of this level of communication would be: "I was really scared when I heard you had a wreck," or, "I love my children, but sometimes I feel I am going crazy when I've been with them all day. I just need a break."

*"Hey, I Hit Something!": Level 5.* In way over your head, your shovel strikes something hard and your heart starts pounding. You dig around the edges, clean off the chest and open it to find the most wonderful treasure you could ever imagine. As you look up to call to your companion, you realize how deep down you really are but feel safe because you see that encouraging smile at the other end. It may actually feel safer for only one person to be digging deep at a time. As one of you becomes vulnerable, it will likely feel safer as the other stands close by being supportive and assuring you of trustworthiness. You can both find the buried treasure of intimacy whether one or both is currently digging deep, because you did it together.

At this level of completely open, truthful communication, true intimacy is reached. This level of communication is absolutely necessary for marriages to stay healthy and strong. All deep relationships, especially marriages, require a foundation of absolute openness and honesty. Although this level definitely presents the greatest level of risk, it also presents the greatest potential for intimacy. As we risk rejection by being vulnerable and allowing others to see us as we really are, we allow the potential for others to accept us unconditionally and without reservation. We are able to move beyond statements like, "If they really knew me they wouldn't like me" to statements like, "Because they really know me, they can accept me as I am." Examples of this level of communications would include: "I'm really afraid that I won't be a good mom because I never had a mom to show me what to do." Or "Please don't leave the room when we are discussing something. That always reminds me of my dad walking out on my mom."

Now that we have looked at the five levels of communication most likely to be used in our interactions, it is time to evaluate at which level you spend most of your time. Throughout any given day, we likely communicate to some extent at each of these levels with people around us, even a spouse. Don't assume that you must always communicate at Level 5 in order to have a thriving marriage. That would be impossible for anyone to sustain, because Level 5 communication takes time and energy that may not always be available. And besides, how deep can a conversation be about who is supposed to take little Johnny to soccer practice Monday night, or whether to have chicken or spaghetti for dinner tonight? Within the marital relationship there is definitely an appropriate place for conversations at Levels 2 and 3. However, Level 1 communication should be minimal. We should not be interacting with a spouse simply out of "social graces or obligations," and we should always be interested in what his or her response will be to our questions. If through your personal evaluation, you realize that you and your spouse practically never communicate at Level 5 but tend to stay at the safer levels such as 1, 2, and 3, then your marriage is likely suffering and intimacy has been lost. It will be important for both of you to begin risking again and sharing feelings that have been kept inside. Depending on how long you have avoided honest sharing and the reasons behind not feeling safe to share, you may need to seek out professional help to begin opening up and taking risks to restore intimacy.

## *Tim and LuAnn's Story*

Tim and LuAnn had only been married 18 months and seemed surprised to be sitting in a counselor's office. LuAnn expressed her concern that Tim was not happy in the marriage and was concerned that he was pulling away from her. She described feeling alone and unimportant to him. "What's wrong? Is it me?" she had asked Tim over and over. To which he always responded "No, I just don't feel like talking. But I'm happy to sit here while you talk." She just couldn't seem to believe that nothing was wrong with him because of his continued refusal to talk to her.

LuAnn described Tim as always having been more on the quiet side, but never to this extent. She used to believe that maybe it was enough that he was happy just to be with her and listen to what she had to say. As time passed and the periods of withdrawal and quietness became more and more frequent, Tim and LuAnn grew further apart. LuAnn often thought to herself, "Eventually he'll figure out that I need him to talk to me too," and "If I keep talking, maybe he'll start." She tried sharing her thoughts and feelings with him, hoping that would spark him to respond with his thoughts and feelings. Tim sat patiently while LuAnn shared her frustrations with work or the kids; he just didn't share his difficulties. LuAnn got so frustrated that she began asking questions and trying to force Tim to talk to her about anything at all. You can probably guess where that landed them. Yep, right in the middle of a big fight. They were talking all right, but the end result was even more distance and hurt feelings.

Once they got in my office and we began talking, what was actually happening became more clear. Tim's natural quietness tended to intensify when he was under stress. When he'd had a rough day at work or had been involved in some creative money management while trying to pay bills, he wanted to be alone and retreated to "think things through." From their premarital counseling, he knew that women (especially LuAnn) needed to talk and feel listened to. So he always made sure to be available to listen about how her day had gone or what she was planning for the weekend. However, he didn't want to bother her with the things that were stressing him. It just didn't seem right to him to vent his stress to her.

Tim never saw this quietness as ignoring LuAnn. He was focusing on handling his stress in a much more positive manner than he remembered his father doing from his childhood. He recalled his father taking out his frustrations about work and money on his mom. He could vividly remember many times when the entire atmosphere of the home would change when Dad sat down to pay bills. Everyone scattered to his or her own room, and before long Dad would be yelling and screaming at Mom about her spending too much money.

Tim had promised himself that he would never treat LuAnn like that. He felt that by dealing with these frustrations on his own he was relieving her of any additional worry about him or money. He never intended for her to feel unimportant. Actually it was just the opposite. She was so important to him that he was trying to protect her from additional stress. He was baffled by her increasing unhappiness in the marriage because he thought just listening to her would help her know she was important to him.

LuAnn, on the other hand, came from a family where both good and bad things were openly discussed. She watched both her mother and father share about their days. She often heard her father discussing his frustrations about his job or money or any other matter that caused stress. Her parents even talked about many of these matters with the children when they were old enough to understand and participate in the conversations. She could recall many times when her parents would sit down together and take turns talking, venting and supporting each other, especially after a bad day. They never seemed to make each other feel bad because they weren't blaming the person they were venting to. They encouraged the children to talk about their thoughts and feelings as well. The silence and retreat she encountered with Tim was foreign to her. And when he did talk to her, it seemed to either be about daily routine things, or what someone had done at work that day, or maybe he would ask a question about what she had just shared with him. He never talked about himself or his feelings. She wanted to know what he thought or felt. In her experience, people who "loved" her talked to her and encouraged her to talk to them. They shared about personal things. So she took Tim's quietness personally and decided, "He must not love me."

As they talked this through, they both became much more aware of the other's perspective and how their behavior was not accomplishing the intended goal of increased satisfaction within the marriage. Tim became more willing and better able to share his thoughts and feelings with LuAnn without fear of being like his father. Once he realized that telling her how he felt or sharing with her about the things he worried about actually made her feel closer to him, it became easier to open up. LuAnn also realized that Tim needed some time to think things through on his own before sharing with her. She learned to not take this as a negative statement about herself, but instead, to see it as Tim's desire to protect her from worrying. There were still times when both Tim and LuAnn would slip back into old patterns, but they were now able to talk about that when it happened.

We can learn many things from Tim and LuAnn's experience. Let's look at a couple of these.

## Advice to Husbands: Just Letting Her Talk Is Not Enough

First, let's take a look at what Tim—and all husbands—need to know about the importance of talking. Although listening is extremely important, it is not the only thing needed to experience the benefits of good communication. The benefits occur when both the husband and wife participate actively in both listening and talking (especially at Levels 4 and 5).

The differences that exist between men and women are evident in just about every area of our lives, and that's especially true when it comes to communication and talking. We all know that stereotypically women are bigger talkers than men and always seem to have something to say. Husbands beware, however. It's not as simple as, "If I let her talk, she'll be happy." When you "let her talk," she needs to feel you are really listening and not just placating her. She doesn't want to feel like she's a commercial break in the middle of the football game—something that's "necessary" to allow the game to be broadcast, but really "unimportant" unless you "need something" like a snack or bathroom break. If you don't listen to her, she will feel unimportant.

Although the woman is most likely to initiate and continue a conversation, she also has a very strong need for someone to talk to her. A woman puts a high value on open, honest communication and often uses this as a measuring stick for how close a relationship is for her. For example, she differentiates between her acquaintances, her friends, and her best friends by the amount of personal sharing that occurs between them. She also measures how much she is worth to her friends by the amount of sharing and disclosing that each friend does with her. Therefore, a woman tends to place low value on relationships that have only minimal (i.e., Levels 1 and 2) communication. And, she experiences a low sense of self worth in a relationship where the other person doesn't openly communicate and share.

In order for your wife to feel highly important to you, you'll need not only to let her talk and actively listen to her, but also—here's the biggie—you'll need to talk to her. This means more than reminding her that you'll be home late from work due to a meeting or telling her as you're washing the truck that you got a raise at work (although those could be good starting points). It means taking time to share with her your thoughts, opinions, and especially your feelings about the things going on in your life. You have to risk being vulnerable and sharing at a Level 4 or 5 in order to build intimacy and a greater sense of satisfaction within marriage.

## *Advice to Wives: Don't Expect Him to Be a Mind Reader*

Okay, now it's your turn, ladies. Let's evaluate what LuAnn—and many of us—needs to learn about improving communication. LuAnn knew that she needed Tim to talk to her, not just about daily things but about things deep inside him. But did she ever communicate that openly to him? No. She thought it to herself, hoped for it, and attempted to get it through modeling it to him. In the end, she was frustrated and dissatisfied and felt unimportant to Tim. How could things have been different if she had just asked for what she needed instead of expecting Tim to read her mind?

If we women love to talk and share from our hearts about personal issues, then why is it that when it comes to our husbands, we expect them to be able to read our minds? Reading minds would mean there is no need to talk. (I don't know about you, but I sure don't want to stop talking, which I'm sure Jim would attest to.) Why do we so often in our closest and most intimate relationship begin to feel that the other person should "just know" what we need, want, think, or feel. And why do we assume they should respond the way we want them to when we don't even tell them what they are responding to?

Mind reading is an expectation most of us seem to hold, although few of us would ever actually admit to it out loud. We would never say to our husbands, "Just read my mind and you will know what to do." How could we? When we are being logical (yes, we are logical at times), we know that this is a completely unrealistic expectation. Mind reading is not a valid form of communication. I have yet to meet a person who is an accurate mind reader. I have met a few couples who have been married for many years and who seem to be able to finish each other's sentences and do seem to "just know" what the other person needs. However, as I examined these relationships closer, I realized that they are not really "mind readers," but simply very observant individuals married to creatures of habit.

Although we seem to know logically that mind reading is not an effective means of communicating or getting our needs met, we tend to feel that it means less if we have to tell him what we need than if he "just knew it." Therefore, one of the most negative results of expecting your husband to be a mind reader is that you are likely to end up disappointed and not getting your needs met. So often I have heard wives say "He should know what I need. If I have to ask for it, then it's not the same." What I say is, "If you don't ask, how is he supposed to know what you need?"

One of the benefits of improving your communication is that you will know and be better able to meet your spouse's needs. When a wife says to me "My husband is just not meeting my needs," my first question back to her is always, "Have you told him what you need?" Usually I hear something like, "No, but he knows. He just refuses to do it." When I ask her husband I find out that he really doesn't know what she needs.

My premise is that if you are expecting him to read your mind and then give you what you need, then you have no basis for complaining when he doesn't respond appropriately or maybe doesn't respond at all. You can expect an unstated need to be met only occasionally and only by luck. However, if you openly ask for what you need, then you can expect that it would be met on a more-frequent-than-not-basis.

Let's say you have had a really rough day and sure could use a hug right now. If you sit there quietly, thinking to yourself, "I hope he comes over here and hugs me," the likelihood of actually getting that hug is slim. You will most likely continue to sit there alone, still upset about your day, and now also upset that your husband is not hugging you. It gets worse, not better, when you expect mind reading.

On the other hand, if you've had a really bad day and sure could use a hug right now, you can say out loud to your husband, "I could really use a hug." Now, the likelihood of getting that hug skyrockets. You end up feeling better, not only from the hug, but also from the fact that your husband heard your need and was willing to meet it.

As we move into the next sections we will be looking at the differences between men and women in conversation as well as ways to nourish or choke our conversations.

## *Differences Between Men and Women*

Let's take a minute to look at just a few of the many differences in perception and communication between men and women.

Men: Summarize a 30-minute phone call down to a 2–5 minute report.
Women: Expand a 30-minute phone call to a 35-minute report.

Men: View questions as a request for information.
Women: View questions as a way to maintain a conversation.

Men: See a "problem" as something that needs to be solved or fixed.
Women: See a "problem" as something that needs to be shared.

Men: "If she wants to know, she'll ask me."
Women: "I can't wait to tell him."

Men: "If she wants to tell me something, she'll tell me without my asking."

Women: "If I don't ask, he will think I don't care."

Men: Life is logical.

Women: Life is emotional.

As you can see, the differences in the way men and women view talking can easily lead to misperceptions and miscommunications. If we continue to relate and respond to our spouse from only our own perspectives, we will likely experience difficulties in the relationship. When your husband doesn't ask about how your day was, you will likely take this as "He doesn't care," because when you care about someone you would ask about his day.

On the other hand, husbands, when your wife shares a problem with you that she's having at work, you automatically step right in with the "solution." That would be the only "logical" response, since the only reason you can imagine her telling you a problem is to have you "fix it." Then you are surprised by her angry response of "Why don't you just listen to how I feel? I can figure out how to fix it later."

The only way to ensure that these misperceptions don't continue to have a negative impact on you and your relationship is to talk openly about them. If you are not sure what your spouse means by a comment, then take the time to ask. If you feel neglected or unimportant, then say that out loud. Using the ECHO conversation technique will help you both avoid misperceptions.

If you truly want to better understand your spouse, you will need to learn how to get him or her to talk to you and how to nourish that conversation once it begins. Often, instead of nourishing a conversation, we end up choking it. By the way we respond, both verbally and nonverbally, we can either "keep them talking" or "shut them up." Although we may say that what we want is to "keep them talking," our responses often do just the opposite. Consider these responses that will choke and eventually kill a conversation.[2]

## *Conversation Chokers*

**Giving Orders:** telling your spouse what to do.

"Stop whining and get back to work!"

"You must ..."

"You have to ..."

"You will ..."

**Making Threats:** telling your spouse what consequences will occur if he or she does a particular thing.

"If you don't tell your mother to mind her own business then I will!"

"You had better _____ if you expect _____."

"If you do that again, I will _____."

**Preaching:** creating a sense of obligation or guilt feelings in the other person.

"You should have called your mother."

"You should have …"

"You ought to …"

"It's your responsibility to …"

**Sending Solutions:** implies your spouse is not able to solve his or her own problems.

"You need to go in tomorrow and ask for a raise."

"What I would do is …"

"Why don't you …"

"You need to …"

**Lecturing or Responding Logically:** trying to influence the person with facts, logic, information, or your own opinions. This is especially choking when your spouse is expressing emotions.

"The fact is that we can't afford to buy a house right now."

"Here's why you are wrong …"

"If you look at this logically, you will see …"

"Yes, but …"

**Criticizing and Blaming:** making a negative evaluation of the person or implying incompetence, poor judgment, or not being "good enough."

"You are not thinking clearly."

"I can't believe you did that."

"It's your fault we're in this mess."

"I never would have …"

**Name-Calling:** putting your spouse into a category and causing him or her to feel unworthy and shameful.

"What makes you think you're so smart?"

"Okay, Mr. Perfect."

"Crybaby."

"Why don't you act your age?"

**Interpreting and Analyzing:** telling your spouse what his or her motives are, or analyzing why he or she is doing or saying something; implying that you know motives better than he or she does.

"You don't really mean that."

"You're just tired"

"What's wrong with you is ..."

**Questioning/Interrogating:** trying to find out reasons, motives or causes; searching for more information to help you solve the problem.

"Why did you ..."

"What made you think ..."

"How could you ..."

**Humoring and Distracting:** attempting to get the person away from the problem or topic, inferring your spouse's problems are unimportant to you.

"Let's talk about more pleasant things."

"Did you know that Mary and Jed are having marital problems too?"[3]

These are responses you will want to avoid! I'm sure you can recall having both sent and received some (if not all) of these at some point in your relationship. We all have struggled with not responding in nourishing ways, but we do not always choose to purposely choke a conversation.

Jeff and Nickie are married and both have full-time jobs outside the home. Nickie has been experiencing some problems with her boss recently and has become very dissatisfied with her work environment. After one particularly difficult day, Nickie comes home practically in tears. She begins to tell Jeff about her no-good, terrible, awful day. While venting her frustrations about how her boss is treating her, she begins to sob.

Understand at this point that Jeff absolutely hates to see his wife hurt and crying. He would do just about anything to make her feel better. Like most men, Jeff is a "fix it" man and very logical overall. He hears the problem Nickie is having at work and he sees how upset she is. He knows he has to help. He mentally changes into his "Super Husband" garb (big blue cape and all) and is ready to come to her rescue. What else can he do? She doesn't appear able to do this herself. So with the best of intentions he begins the "fixing" process. He tells her exactly what she should do first thing tomorrow morning and how to best handle her boss. To his surprise, Nickie does not act at all thankful for this rescue attempt. She doesn't immediately stop crying. As a matter of fact, she becomes more upset and seems to move from being angry with her boss to being angry with him. *What did I do? I was trying to help,* is all he can think.

Nickie is frustrated that Jeff was not listening to her share about her no-good, terrible, awful day. He was more interested in how to fix it. She is thinking to herself, "Doesn't he think I'm smart enough to figure out what to do? If I needed his advice I would have asked for it. Why can't he just understand how I'm feeling?" At this point, even if his advice is a good idea, she probably won't use it, but will instead come up with an alternative on her own just to prove that she can.

As you can see, Jeff's intentions are good. But in using conversation chokers as his way of responding, he actually gets the opposite of what he hopes for.

## *Advice to Husbands*

When your wife is highly emotional, it is important to kick in the ECHO conversation skills from the previous chapter. Wait until she has expressed her emotions and feels you have heard and understood her. Then you may be surprised that she has moved into a more logical mindset. At this point, and not before, she will be able to come up with possible solutions herself or to hear what solutions you have in mind. If you offer these too soon, they will be lost in a flood of hurt feelings. Be patient. Since you are not emotionally involved, you may be able to see a solution before she does; however, she will feel more supported by you if you just listen and wait for her to ask for what she needs.

Now that we have identified those responses that can choke a conversation, you should have an idea of what kinds of things not to do or say. But what should you do? In this next section you will learn how to keep a conversation going for hours, by nourishing it with breaths of life.

## *How to Nourish a Conversation*

Have you ever been in a conversation that just seemed to die out before it even got started? Or maybe you've tried to talk to a person who you could just tell was not interested in what you had to say? On the other hand, have you ever walked away from talking to someone and thought to yourself, *Wow, I think I could have talked to her for hours and told her anything.* What's the difference? Most likely, it's that person's verbal and nonverbal communications that made the difference. Let's look at some things that you can do to help your spouse feel he or she could talk to you for hours and tell you anything.

*1. Use door openers.* These are open, noncoercive invitations to talk. Often you can tell by the way a person is acting that he or she might want to talk but may be reluctant. If this person is your spouse, draw him or her out gently. Open the door and make yourself available by giving an invitation to talk to you. This can make it easier to share because you took the first step by showing interest. Some examples of door openers are: "Would you like to talk?" "I'm here if you would like someone to talk to." "I sense that something might be bothering you." "I'd like to know what you think."

*2. Demonstrate open and attentive body posture.* The nonverbal communication of body posture can be powerful. You communicate interest and attentiveness through your body by facing the person who is speaking, leaning slightly forward, and keeping your arms open. You can communicate nonacceptance and a lack of interest by turning your body away (even slightly), leaning back, and crossing your arms in front of your body.

*3. Make good eye contact.* Another important nonverbal communication is eye contact. Positioning yourself so that you can make good eye contact and then doing it shows interest and will likely help keep your spouse talking. The amount of eye contact should be comfortable and appropriate. If it is constant or intense you may be communicating that you are being disapproving, critical, or judgmental. However, if there is little or no eye contact you may be communicating lack of interest.

*4. Use occasional encouragers.* If you want something to happen, it usually helps to encourage it. If you want a conversation to continue and your spouse to keep sharing thoughts and feelings, then you should encourage him or her to do so without distracting from the communication. How do you do that? Through the occasional use of encouragers. These are brief indicators that let your spouse know that you are interested and following the conversation. Sprinkled throughout the conversation, these statements and actions encourage the speaker to continue. "Tell me more." "Yes." Nodding your head; "Really?" "For instance ..." "Uh-huh." "I see."

*5. Listen; really listen, using ECHO conversation skills.* Be sure to repeat back to your spouse what you heard, especially the feelings he or she seems to be experiencing. Be careful to do this only after your spouse has stopped talking to avoid interrupting. (See previous chapter for more on this topic.)

*6. Use open-ended questions.* These questions are designed for the purpose of drawing out the person you are talking to. Used sparingly, they will often help the speaker sort out thoughts and feelings more thoroughly. Most people tend to use closed-ended questions that serve to cut a conversation short and often come across as if you know how the other person feels or what the person should do. Closed-ended questions usually require only a one- or two-word answer. In contrast, open-ended questions tend to request further elaboration on the topic. Here are some examples of both open and closed-ended questions:

Avoid: "Did that make you angry?"
Instead: "How did that make you feel?"

Avoid: "Was it a horrible experience?"
Instead: "What was it like for you?"

Avoid: "Don't you think you should tell your parents?"
Instead: "How do you think you should handle that situation?"

*7. Focus on the relationship.* In the process of a conversation, remember that the goal is to increase intimacy. In other words, the conversation, the act of talking, the sharing of thoughts and feelings, causes the increased sense of connection between the two of you. However, we often can get distracted by the topic, and even more often by the solution. When this happens, we lose track of the importance of the connection. The most important part of a sharing time is not the solution, but the feeling of intimacy. Level 4 and 5 conversations are not necessarily solution-based. Although they may be working toward a solution at times, it is more important that they include sharing for as long as necessary. Once a solution is presented, the conversation tends to be over. So remember if your goal is to feel closer to your spouse, be careful to hold off on the solution until the sharing is completed.

Before we move into the application section of this chapter and get you actually doing some of what you have just learned, let's take just a minute to highlight the chapter. This will serve as a quick reference to the steps necessary for improved talking skills.

1. Make talking to your spouse a priority. Pencil it into your daily schedule if necessary.
2. Remember that talking is the number one way to build intimacy in a marriage.
3. Take time to gather your thoughts and feelings before sharing.
4. Work toward Level 4 and 5 communication on a regular basis with your spouse.
5. Remember the differences in the way the men and women communicate, and adjust your presentation and your expectations to allow for these.
6. Avoid the expectation of mind reading.
7. Actively use techniques that nourish conversation and avoid those that tend to choke the conversation.

## *Application*

What good does it do to read and learn all this stuff if you don't apply it in some way that actually benefits your relationship? Thus, the importance of homework and application.

*Fish Bowl Conversations.* The goal here is to get the two of you talking to each other. This may not be as easy as it seems. Often I have sent couples home with the assignment to "Talk to each other," and they come back the next week saying something like, "We tried, but every time we would sit down to talk one of us would say, 'Okay, what do you want to talk about?' and the other would say 'I don't know, what do you want to talk about?' and on and on. We couldn't seem to come up with a starting point." They often ended up frustrated, and the conversation stopped before it ever got started.

The most difficult part of talking often is simply getting started. You can find a list of 100 Conversation Starters at the end of the chapter. One of the best ways to use this list is to cut the topics apart and put them in a fish bowl. When you have set aside time to talk, or when you just happen to have a little extra time, one of you draws a topic out of the fish bowl and the discussion begins. Both of you address the topic before drawing out the next one. The assignment is a fun way not only to get the conversations going, but also to learn some things about your spouse you may never have known before. The more you know about a person, the more intimate the relationship becomes. Feel free to add in some topics of your own as well. (You can easily adapt this assignment to use with the whole family by choosing and adding topics the children can be involved in. It can be a great car trip or family night activity for the whole family to learn more about each other.)

# 100 Conversation Starters

Where do you see yourself in 5, 10, 20 years?

Describe your most romantic evening.

If money were no issue where would you like to travel?

If the house caught on fire and all your family were safe and you had time to save five things, what five things would you save?

If you inherited $100,000, what would you do with it?

What would be the first thing you would buy if you won the lottery?

What is your biggest regret?

What was your most embarrassing moment?

Describe a perfect evening.

How would you define love?

Tell me about a special childhood memory.

What was your favorite Christmas and why?

What did your parents teach you about marriage?

Share a sad memory with me.

What things are you looking forward to this week, month, and year?

What do you like most about your job?

Tell me about your talents.

Tell me something you are afraid of.

How would you like to spend a day alone?

Plan the perfect date.

If you could change one thing about yourself, what would it be? Why?

What do you like best about yourself?

What do you like best about me? Why?

What is one of your favorite memories about us?

What do you remember most about our dating?

What do you remember most about our wedding or honeymoon?

What could I do to please you more sexually?

If you could be any animal, what would you be? Why?

How would you like to see the household responsibilities divided?

What do you think heaven will be like?

Tell me about your salvation experience.

Tell me about a spiritual high point in your life.

Tell me about a spiritual low point in your life.

What is the best advice you ever received?

If you could have three wishes, what would they be?

How can I show you that I love you?

Tell me about a time when God answered a prayer.

What makes you laugh?

Tell me your favorite joke.

What was your favorite grade in school? Why?

How often would you like to make love?

Is there a difference between making love and sex? Explain.

Share a fantasy with me.

What advice would you give a friend about to get married?

Would you rather vacation in the mountains, at the ocean, or a big city? Why?

What was your favorite fairy tale growing up?

What kind of movies do you enjoy?

Would you rather spend a quiet evening with just the two of us; with one other couple; or, at a social gathering of several couples? Why?

Would you rather be smart, beautiful, or famous? Explain.

When was the last time you cried?

If there had never been original sin, what do you think the world would be like?

After salvation, what do you pray for most for our children?

If you could have picked anyone in the world to be your parents, who would you have picked?

Where would you like to live?

What do we want to teach our children about marriage?

Do you think we fight fair?

How could we improve on our conflict resolution skills?

What would you consider to be your top five priorities in life?

What do you think my top five priorities are?

What are you feeling right now?

What are you thinking about right now?

What does intimacy mean?

What strengths do you see in me?

What expectations did you have coming into marriage?

Which marital expectations were met and which were not met?

What would we do if our TV were out of order for one week?

How did you decide on your career?

What is the best part of our relationship currently?

What is romance?

Do you see me as a better giver or receiver? Explain.

What is your favorite recreational activity?

What is something we have never done together that you would like us to try?

What size box does the "perfect gift" come in? What would be inside?

List five of your "favorites."

Describe your dream house.

If for one day you could be anyone who ever lived, who would you choose?

What's your most memorable childhood experience?

Would you rather travel by car, plane, boat, or train? Why?

What question would you like to ask God once you are in heaven?

What one experience would you like to be sure to have before you die?

What's the craziest thing you have ever done in public?

If you could choose any career what would you be?

How can I make love to you without intercourse?

If you could spend a day with anyone who ever lived, who would you choose? Why?

Who would you like to visit once in heaven?

What "impossible" experience would you like to have?

What is a recreational activity that you have never tried but would like to?

Tell me two things you "want" from me and two things you "need" from me.

If you could have lived in any time period, which would you have picked?

Who has been the biggest positive influence in your life? Explain.

Tell me about your best friend in high school.

Tell me about your first date.

Where is the most adventurous place you would consider making love?

What was the happiest time of your life?

If you were a writer what would you write?

If you could trade lives with someone for a week who would you trade with and why?

What is the hardest thing for you to understand about the opposite sex?

What is your favorite movie and why?

What do you worry about?

Name three things I used to do for you that you enjoyed that I have not done for awhile.

# "And the Winner Is . . ."

## The Art of Conflict Management

> "*A* gentle answer turns away wrath,
> but a harsh word stirs up anger."
> *Proverbs 15:1*

Do you remember Matt and Laura from the fairy tale in chapter 1? They fell in love after finding the treasure box and the warm fuzzies inside. Then when the warm fuzzies were misplaced, cold pricklies invaded their lives at an ever-increasing rate.

One day early in their relationship, Matt and Laura were walking hand-in-hand, sharing thoughts and dreams for the future. They had been exchanging warm fuzzies for quite some time now and felt closer than ever. They both knew they wanted to spend the rest of their lives together.

As they moved past a glade of trees, there in the opening they saw an unusual structure. Seemingly out of nowhere, there stood a large square platform ringed with ropes around the edges. It had been a long time since either of them had seen one of these.

Laura recalled standing beside a structure like this and watching her parents fight. Sometimes these events would be short and mild. But she recalled a few incidents where the battle seemed to go on for days and became brutal. At the end of every encounter a voice from nowhere would proclaim, "And the winner is … ." This was always followed by one of her parent's names, and the "winner" would puff up and walk away proudly as if having won a trophy. The other parent would walk away slowly, wounded and hurting.

Matt also had memories of this type of a structure. He recalled being in the ring with several different people—his brother, the bully down the road, a recent boss. He had no pleasant memories of this place and recalled not feeling good even if that anonymous voice had declared him "the winner." Even as the winner, he felt wounded when he left.

As Matt and Laura silently played back these memories, both wondered, *Why is this here now?* They could never imagine the two of them in this fighting ring together. They went back to their conversation about hopes and dreams of the future. As Laura shared her personal dream of building a home next door to her mother and how much help her parents could be with children once they came along, Matt found himself surprised and confused. This was not what he had in mind! And before they knew it, they were standing right in the middle of the ring.

Their verbal sparring was not nearly as comfortable as sharing hopes and dreams. They both wanted to have their say, even if it meant talking right over the other. They interrupted each other, and at one point, Laura completely turned her back on Matt and planned to leave the ring. But she couldn't find the way out. Eventually, Matt decided the fight wasn't worth the trouble and gave in to Laura's plans and ideas. But he didn't feel good. This had been the biggest cold prickly he had felt from Laura, and he wanted to get away.

And then the voice came, "And the winner is … Laura!"

Laura was pleased that she had won, but she also wanted to move away from the ring as soon as possible. Once they were away, Laura suggested they exchange their warm fuzzies. They did, and they both began to feel better.

During the early stages of their relationship, Matt and Laura found themselves thrown into the ring from time to time, often without warning. They seemed to "win" equally often. Although they didn't enjoy these times, neither felt overwhelmed because they were still getting more warm fuzzies than cold pricklies. The warm fuzzies helped them not only heal more quickly but also continue to grow closer and closer in spite of periodic visits to the fighting ring.

As time passed, their encounters in the fighting ring became more frequent and less mild. The punches they threw became more damaging, and they started hitting below the belt. Their words became weapons, like swords that cut deep into the other person. Sometimes the injuries were so deep that even exchanging warm fuzzies didn't help. Even worse, sometimes they didn't even want to exchange warm fuzzies. Instead, they just went to separate corners to attend to their wounds. Although the voice continued to announce the "winner" at the end of each encounter, they began to realize this didn't feel like winning.

One day Matt decided to try something different. He needed to tell Laura something that was bothering him, but every time he had tried to do so, they ended up in the middle of the fighting ring. He thought that maybe they could avoid the ring if he told her he wanted to talk instead of what he's always done—wait until he was getting angry then throw the first punch.

Once he decided how he wanted to do this, he called Laura from work. He gently said, "I've been feeling bothered about something and wondered if we could make some time to talk. Would you be available later tonight?" He was expecting Laura to respond defensively, but this time was different. Laura responded pleasantly saying, "Sure, that sounds fine. How about around 8:30?" The time was set and no one seemed upset—at least not yet.

That evening they sat down to talk. As they began, they found themselves walking toward the ring. Matt immediately said, "Wait, this is what I was trying to avoid!" Then he realized something was different. They were walking toward the ring—not thrown right in the middle of it like in the past. Neither was feeling angry.

As they approached the platform, they noticed something they had never seen before. There was an entrance into the ring. If there was an entrance, there must be an exit as well. They knew it would feel more comfortable going in knowing they could get out. They climbed the few stairs to the top of the platform, and noticed something else they had never seen—a plaque.

The writing on the plaque was the same as that on the paper in their treasure box. The last time they saw that writing, it had given them words of wisdom that caused them to feel closer than ever. As they read, they hoped the same would be true this time. The plaque read:

You are about to enter the Ring of Resolution. Inside there exists an opportunity to grow closer and increase intimacy through your conflict by adhering to a few simple rules.
**Be open and honest,**
**Be gentle with words,**
**Be willing to listen,**
**Then there's no need for swords.**

**You are fighting for intimacy,**
**This much is true,**
**When it's all said and done,**
**Winners or Losers will be two.**

WARNING:
This is the only true entrance into the Ring of Resolution. If you find yourself inside without first passing this way you are in grave danger. The Voice of Deception will judge the battle and announce a "winner." But heed the words of truth and know that both have lost.

If these rules are broken, you risk damaging yourself, your mate, and the relationship between you. As you enter, you MUST agree to abide by the rules and to fight fair.

Matt and Laura paid particular attention to the warning because they had experienced the importance of warnings from the paper in their warm fuzzy treasure box.

Why had they never seen these rules before? Probably because they were breaking most of them and focusing on coming out on top. There had to be a winner, didn't there? Not according to this plaque. It said that either both win more intimacy or both lose it. That was exactly what had happened in the past. They always heard the "Voice of Deception" announce a winner at the end of their battles. Yet, they both seem to walk away feeling like they had lost.

Now they began to understand. They were hurting each other and the relationship when they allowed themselves to be thrown into the ring. But if they could choose to enter the ring and abide by the rules, they could grow closer through a resolution. They had tried to avoid coming to the ring at all, but that never seemed to work for long. Things built up and eventually the battle would begin. They had found that the longer they avoided the ring, the more damaging the next battle would be. They both came to the next battle with more weapons.

As they read the plaque again, they realized it didn't give any instructions about avoiding the ring, just how to act once there. They knew they needed to learn the rules to avoid further damage to their relationship.

Matt and Laura reviewed the rules one last time before going in. They walked to center ring and sat down facing each other. They were amazed at the comfort they felt. They addressed the issue Matt had asked to discuss and followed the rules. At the end of the discussion they felt they had reached a resolution that both agreed would help alleviate the problem.

Wow! It really was possible to resolve a problem without all the punches and cutting words. As they walked out of the ring hand-in-hand, they realized they had not heard a voice announcing the winner. And then they realized why. There was no need for a judge because they both knew who had won. They had.

## Why a Whole Chapter on Fighting?

In marriage, both partners win or both partners lose. "Winning" is having a growing relationship that provides intimacy and satisfaction and lasts for a lifetime. Every chapter of this book has focused on building intimacy. Although some relationships may last for a lifetime, they are not all described as satisfactory or intimate by the parties involved. Several researchers have studied long-standing relationships to try to identify what exactly it is that separates the satisfied from the dissatisfied couples. And one major answer tends to surface every time: constructive problem solving, or conflict resolution skills.[1]

Let's get real here, all of us are going to have our disagreements — even fights. We are humans, and each one of us is different from the next one. We have different personalities, opinions, and feelings. And most of us like to express our personal thoughts and opinions to those closest to us. Since it is impossible that you are exactly like your spouse, then it is also impossible to totally avoid your differences. It is not the presence or absence or the magnitude of the differences between the partners that is the problem. Rather, it is how you handle the differences. Research shows that couples who are able to successfully resolve their differences have the best chance to have a long-term, successful marriage.[2] In other words, happy couples have developed various healthy ways of handling the inevitable conflict. Unhappy couples probably have not. So if the goal of this book is to help you build the strongest relationship possible, then it would make sense to devote at least one whole chapter to learning how to fight fairly. The win-win result comes when a couple is able to resolve a disagreement together and thus create a deeper understanding and respect between themselves.

I once heard Pastor Tony Evans speak about the topic of conflicts in marriage. One of the points he made was that it's not the good times of the relationship that define the relationship. All couples can look good when life is smooth. It is the couple's response to the storms of life that shows what they are really made of. We know that the storms of life will come into every marriage. That's when our true colors show. It is especially important at this point in a relationship that both spouses have their lives firmly built on the foundation of Jesus Christ. Without that firm foundation, the storms of life will likely blow your relationship to pieces.

## Sirens Going Off

"Isn't it wrong to be angry with my spouse?" Absolutely not! Anger is simply a feeling. Feelings are neither right nor wrong, they are just feelings. And unless you are a robot or other inanimate object, you cannot avoid feeling anger at some point in your relationship. Of course some of us experience it more often than others, but the experience of anger in a relationship is not wrong. The Bible addresses the emotion of anger specifically, and nowhere does it say, "do not feel angry." In both Psalms 4:4 and Ephesians 4:26, Scripture says, "In your anger, do not sin." The assumption here is that you will feel anger, and when you do, you are called to not sin. So feeling angry is not the problem. It does not mean that you don't love each other. It does not mean that either of you is "bad." It only means that you are human. By saying and believing that it is wrong to feel angry within a marriage, you set an unrealistic expectation for you and your spouse and likely doom your relationship for failure.

Conflict is a part of any relationship, and is often the result of the natural differences present between two people whose needs are unmet. Anger can be a warning sign that something is wrong in the relationship or that conflicts are not being resolved.

I sometimes think of anger as being like the tornado siren in our neighborhood. Its blaring is unexpected, and it can be very loud depending on how close you are to it. It signals that danger is imminent. Although it can evoke feelings of fear, anxiety, or even panic, it almost always causes us to take action. We are moved to evaluate the situation and become aware of the potential destruction that could be right around the corner. We take this warning seriously and immediately do what we can to avoid harm to ourselves and loved ones.

I don't think any of us would view the tornado siren going off as "wrong." Even though it may make us uncomfortable, we are thankful that it is there to help us prepare for and avoid injury. Neither is the anger in a relationship wrong. Instead we should use it as a sign that something is posing a danger. Use anger as a signal that something needs to change and then move to correct and resolve the problem as soon as possible.

The rest of this chapter will focus on how to correct and resolve the problems within your relationship to decrease the amount of anger you experience. You will learn how to fight in a way that doesn't destroy intimacy, but rather actually builds it. You will learn both what to do and what not to do in this process of fair fighting. So let's get started.

## *How to Have a F.A.I.R. Fight*

Let's look at the essential components of F.A.I.R. fighting.

**F. Forgiving Attitude**

**A. Apply ECHO Conversation Skills**

**I. "I" Messages**

**R. Resolution**

## *F*

### *Forgiving Attitude*

You may be wondering why this is the first key component. Doesn't forgiveness come at the end, after all the hurt and pain of a fight? Or maybe I put it first just to make the "F.A.I.R." acronym work out? Neither of these is accurate. Forgiveness comes as the first component because it is the most important. (But it sure didn't hurt that F.A.I.R. started with an F.) You must be willing to forgive even before the conflict begins. Remember the old saying, "Sticks and stones may break my bones, but words will never hurt me." How untrue! A quote I saw on a church sign applies here: "If the tongue is so light, why is it that no man can seem to hold it?" Most often the words we say do the most damage to our spouse. So it's important to carefully watch what we say during a disagreement. And an attitude of forgiveness at the beginning of a disagreement may actually help avoid the hurts and pains that could come later.

Imagine, before the conflict begins, saying to yourself, *I know we are about to enter into a difficult discussion. I know that we both want to see this resolved. But because we are human, and we make mistakes, I know that either one of us may say something hurtful. I know we are both trying to avoid doing this, but if we do slip up, I know I am willing to forgive my spouse or to ask for forgiveness and do my best to move on.* Do you think you would enter the discussion with a different perspective? Just maybe your attitude would soften and the possible slip-ups would not seem quite so harmful. I know that the attitude I enter a discussion with is usually intensified as the discussion continues. If I start out defensive, I seem to hear things in a more negative light and I become more defensive. However, if I enter with a softness and willingness to forgive, I seem better able to hear what Jim is trying to say, and better able to look past things that may come out wrong.

An important point here is to avoid assigning motives to your spouse's statements. This may be difficult to do. Once we have entered into a conflict, we often become self-protective. We believe that there are good reasons for our own behavior. If we make a mistake in how we say something, we respond with "I didn't mean that." And, of course, we expect our spouse to forget our mistake and move on. After all, it wasn't intentional, right? However, we usually don't give that same benefit of the doubt to our spouse. Somehow in our minds we often assign an evil motive or a bad attitude as the reason for his or her behavior. And if he or she says something in a way that hurts us, we just know it was "on purpose." Beware: this "self-protective" approach usually becomes "self-defeating" in the fight for greater intimacy.

In the past, out of your anger, one or both of you may have said things to purposely hurt the other. Hopefully this will become a thing of the past as you learn to resolve conflicts instead of just fighting. As you work on these skills, an attitude of forgiveness and an understanding that your spouse is not intentionally trying to hurt you will help you keep your fights F.A.I.R.

If either of you becomes hurtful in a conflict, it is essential that you admit this and actively seek your spouse's forgiveness. This means to actually put your mistake and apology into words and ask your spouse to forgive you (e.g., "I am sorry that I compared you to your mother; that was wrong. Please forgive me."). Don't just say, "I'm sorry" and assume he or she knows what you are apologizing for. Remember also to grant forgiveness verbally.

# A

*Apply ECHO Conversation Skills*

The second key component to F.A.I.R. fighting is the ability to listen to what is being said. My hope is that you have been practicing this skill on a regular basis on general topics and conversations. If you haven't, I would suggest that you review chapter 5 before moving on.

Listening and repeating back what you hear your spouse say on a fairly neutral topic is one thing, but attempting to do this on a topic that the two of you disagree on is an entirely different experience. You probably already know from past experience how hard it is to simply hear someone saying something you don't agree with. Just imagine how much harder it would be to say those words back. You would be saying with your own mouth words that are not yours and that you don't agree with. Even worse, you have to do it without correcting them or adding your opinion. You need to be able to repeat back what you heard without exaggerating the other person's gestures or tone (which we often do unintentionally out of our own emotions). Talk about hard! So be sure you get the skills down well before trying to use them in a conflict situation. (There is an exercise to help you with this in the Application section of this chapter.)

Conversations usually escalate to arguments and then end up unresolved if one or both parties did not feel heard or understood. The goal here is for both you and your spouse to feel heard and understood, and ECHOing can accomplish that goal. Understanding does not necessarily mean agreeing. Your focus should not be on getting your spouse to agree with you when you are in a conflict. Rather, it should be on getting each of you to understand what the other is thinking and feeling. You may never agree, but you will most likely be able to gain some understanding of the other's point of view. ECHO conversations will help you clarify what's being said and identify the true issues you need to address. Once that is accomplished, the possible solutions to the real issues seem easier to find and greater intimacy results. As you apply these skills of F.A.I.R. fighting, seek more to understand than to be understood. ECHOing will help you accomplish that.

# 1

## *"I" Messages*

"I" messages are one of the best ways to express anger (or any feeling) appropriately. When you use "I" messages, you don't attack the other person in a dirty, mud-slinging, win-at-all-costs battle. Instead, you simply express your own feelings about a situation ("I feel neglected when you ignore me"). These are your feelings and yours only and therefore, cannot be challenged by others. When you use "I" statements, you take responsibility for your feelings. You don't blame or judge the other person for making you feel this way ("You always ignore me! You don't even care about me!").

"I" messages are made up of a description of how you feel, followed by a description of what is happening when you feel that way. An "I" message should take the following form: "I feel (your emotion) when (description of the circumstances)." "I" messages not only help us identify our feelings and make us responsible for them, but they also empower us. In other words, they help us realize that we are not helpless or powerless to change things. "You" messages, in contrast, make others responsible for our feelings, blame others for the problem, and therefore make us helpless to bring about changes. Blaming is a big part of making "you" statements. Blaming not only puts responsibility for the problem on the other person but also responsibility for the solution. When you blame others you are saying, "Since the problem is your fault, then only you can change it." We tend to want to blame others, while seeing ourselves as blameless (most likely untrue). The problem with this is that you also end up seeing yourself as helpless to resolve the situation (also probably untrue). Let's look at a few examples of "you" vs. "I" statements. As we do this, try to evaluate how you may be using "you" messages to blame or judge your spouse, or to avoid taking responsibility for your own feelings.

"You make me so mad"
"I feel angry when you _____."
"You are a lazy, good-for-nothing, jerk."
"I feel taken advantage of when you don't help out around the house."
"You had better stop flirting."
"I feel insecure in our relationship when you flirt."
"All you ever do is spend money."
"I feel nervous when you spend money before the bills are paid."

# R

*Resolution*

The final key concept of F.A.I.R. fighting is the importance of reaching a resolution. So often conflicts are started but never really finished. Why is that? Reasons include (but are not limited to): walking away, getting sidetracked, bringing up irrelevant topics, throwing up past events, natural interruptions, etc. The result of unresolved conflict is harbored anger and frustration for one or both parties.

Take the following example and consider how often something like this happens in your relationship. You start a discussion about a particular topic (e.g., "Why didn't you call and tell me you were going to be late?"); defensiveness is evident and conflict begins ("I tried to call ..."); another topic is introduced ("... but I couldn't get through because you were on the Internet like you always are"); now both parties are defensive and another topic is added ("Well, maybe I wouldn't be on the Net so much if you were ever here to talk to"); and on and on it goes. Where it will stop no one knows. But very likely one or both of you will withdraw or walk away. All of these irrelevant topics that get introduced are unresolved conflicts from the past. Not only does everyone involved become hurt and angry, but now you have completely lost track of the original issue, which simply becomes one more of the many other topics that are unresolved and therefore, now available to be thrown up in the next conflict.

Do your best to keep the conversation focused on the original topic until it has been adequately resolved. Then, and only then, move on to additional topics that you may need to address. Be careful here, however, not to overload your spouse with grievances. Now that you have the skills to resolve conflicts, these can be handled a couple at a time until eventually you can reach a place where there are no unresolved issues to bring up.

When emotions begin to escalate to the point that either of you is unable to be civil and rational, then call a time-out. Either party can call a time-out, and it should be used for the purpose of calming down. This is not an escape route. It is simply a break in the conversation. Agree on a time to reconvene and continue the discussion once both of you have had some time apart and can think about the topic more reasonably. The amount of time apart will vary depending on the level of emotions. It may be as little as 10 minutes, but I would suggest it not be longer than 24 hours. The longer you wait, the less likely it will be that you actually come back to the topic and resolve it. Use this time to appropriately release any excessive emotions. Take advantage of physical safety valves (such as walking, jogging, cleaning, or other physical activity) or emotional safety valves (such as crying, journaling, or praying). Once you feel your emotions are back in line, focus on what you think and feel about the topic and how you would like to see it resolved. When the time-out is over, you will be ready to continue the discussion to resolution.

Now that you understand the four key components to F.A.I.R. fighting, it's time to look at the specific rules that will help make these concepts a reality in your marriage. You'll need to agree on some basics in order for your conflicts to proceed toward the point of resolution and greater intimacy. You will also learn in the application section of this chapter how to personalize your own list of "Rules for F.A.I.R. Fighting" that will apply specifically to your marriage.

## Rules for F.A.I.R. Fighting

*1. Clearly identify the problem or issue.* Be specific when you introduce a problem. This helps avoid the often-asked question, "What are we fighting about, anyway?" Be brief and objective in your description of the problem. Fight the urge to exaggerate. Examples of being clear and specific would include: "I want to discuss the credit card bill that shows $300 spent for clothes." Or, "I feel angry when you don't clean up the dishes after dinner like we agreed."

*2. Don't just complain, no matter how specific you are; ask for a reasonable change that will relieve the problem.* This is one my husband has always lived by. He has used it in his managing and supervising of various companies, as well as in our home. You'll often hear him say "Don't present me with a problem or gripe unless you have thought of at least one possible solution." Be sure to ask for practical, possible, and fair changes. Avoid making outrageous demands. Don't ask for changes regarding things your spouse cannot change (e.g., body build, intelligence, and basic personality) and avoid being vague in your request. For example, don't say, "Don't be so mean." Instead, say, "Don't call me names."

*3. Always be willing to compromise.* Be aware that the one possible solution you have come up with may not be the only or even the best way to resolve the conflict. Remember that your partner's view of reality and the problem will be just as real as yours. Therefore, at the end of the discussion, it may not be your original solution that is the agreed upon final solution. Write down the final solution, date it, and sign it with both signatures. Include a trial period for trying out the agreement, followed by a predetermined time to evaluate again.

*4. Confine yourself to one issue at a time.* Be specific, limited, and direct with your concern. Don't overload your partner with several grievances at once. To do this only serves to make him or her feel hopeless and suggests that you have either been hoarding complaints or that you have not thought through what is really bothering you. Be careful not to switch to another issue while the first is still unresolved. You need to stay on the subject in order to reach resolution. Do not bring in unrelated grievances for the purpose of making a stronger point.

*5. Arrange a specific time and place to work it through.* If at all possible, agree upon a time you can discuss the issue without interruption. Be sure to schedule enough time to avoid feeling rushed. Don't bring up an issue when you know your partner is especially tired or nervous or when he or she is walking out the door. Also be sure not to choose to bring up the issue at an embarrassing time, such as in front of friends. You need to be willing to turn off the TV and the phone and give each other your undivided attention. It is also helpful when you are setting the time that you identify the topic to be discussed. This allows both of you to come to the discussion having put some thought into the topic. You could say something like, "I need to share my feelings about _____ and see if we can come up with some possible changes. Could you be available tomorrow night after the kids are in bed?"

*6. Attack the problem, not the person.* It is important to dwell on behaviors, not on personality or characteristics. Never put labels on your spouse. If you really believed that your spouse was incompetent or suffered from some hopeless basic flaw, you probably wouldn't be with him or her. Don't make sweeping or labeling judgments about feelings, especially about whether or not they are real or important. Don't tell your spouse that he or she is "wrong." If you do, you can be assured that your "wrong" spouse will fight even harder to prove that he or she is "right."

*7. Avoid using absolutes. Never say "never."* The use of words like "always," "never," "every time," "everything," and so on will almost always result in a defensive response from your spouse. He or she will undoubtedly be able to recall the one (and I'm sure the only one) exception to whatever statement you just made. The battle to prove each other wrong will be off and running and a resolution will likely not be reached.

*8. Never assume.* I mean never assume anything. (Yes, I am using an absolute, but we are not in a conflict right now.) Don't assume that you know what your partner is thinking or feeling. Don't assume or predict how he or she will react or say or accept or reject. Never assume that your partner knows what you are thinking or feeling. Avoid mind reading; instead, be sure that both of you are completely honest and open in expressing your own thoughts and feelings.

*9. Forget the past and stay with the here and now.* Try not to drag up, "I remember when you ..." Don't bring up old hurts and mistakes committed by your spouse. The Bible says, "He who covers over an offense promotes love, but whoever repeats the matter separates close friends" (Proverbs 17:9). Covering an offense refers to forgiving and agreeing not to bring it up again. It may be tempting when you are hurt and angry to remind your spouse of something from the past. But true love will keep its mouth shut! What either of you did last night, last month, or last year is not as important as what you are doing or feeling right now. Bring up hurts, grievances, and irritations at the very earliest moment. Do not save these up as extra ammunition for the next battle.

*10. Admit when you are wrong.* Be graciously silent when you are right. You should be able to recognize a legitimate complaint and handle it appropriately. When you are right, don't "rub it in." Resist the temptation to say, "I told you so."

*11. Think before you speak.* Take time to consult your real thoughts and feelings before speaking. Definitely do this at the beginning of a discussion, but also periodically throughout the discussion to avoid making impulsive, inaccurate statements. Don't be afraid to take a minute to close your eyes and sort out your thoughts before continuing.

12. *Don't hit below the belt.* Blows above the belt can be absorbed. However, blows below the belt are intolerable and unfair. Avoid criticizing the unchangeable and pushing on those old sore-spots. Know your partner's emotional limits and stay within those limits. Everyone has an "Achilles' heel," and aiming there could be fatal to the relationship. Be sure to measure the size of your weapon against the seriousness of the issue before taking aim and firing.

13. *Be ready and willing to forgive.* When all is said and done, you need to be able to put the incident behind you. Forgive each other and appreciate that each of you were willing to work toward resolution of the issue and remained within the F.A.I.R. fighting rules.

14. *Apply ECHO Conversation Skills.* Be sure to ask for and give feedback of the major points to assure that you feel heard and that you understand what your spouse wants or needs. Focus on what he or she is saying, not on what you are going to say next.

15. *Use "I" messages, not "You" messages.* "I" messages allow you to present your grievance in a nonattacking way. "I feel ..." elicits your spouse's sympathy, whereas "you should ..." elicits an angry defense. "I" messages make it clear that you accept responsibility for your feelings. "You" messages usually come across as blaming, judging, or condemning, all of which will put your partner on the defensive.

## *Finding the Value in These New Skills*

No matter what skill you are trying to learn, you must at some point determine the skill to be of some value to you or you will not continue to practice, use, and master it. We talked in chapter 2 about the different stages of new skill acquisition (i.e., initial learning, awkward use, conscious application, and natural use). In order for you to practice and struggle through these stages to the point of reaching natural use, you must deem the new skill as having value to you. Remember Taffeta's experience of learning to ride her new bike? This was definitely a struggle and hard work for her, but she saw this skill as having great value. In her eyes, it was going to increase her mobility, freedom, and recreation. As a matter of fact, she knew that if she got really good at it, she could probably even beat her best friend in a race to the park. To her it was all worth the struggle.

The skills you're learning through this book are much the same. In order to put in the hard work and struggle through the stages of learning these new skills, you must at some point decide if they will be of value to you.

Let me share with you an example of how one couple learned the value of the skills of communication and conflict management. Brett and Juli had been married about six years. Brett worked full time in a factory setting, and Juli worked full time as a stay-at-home mom. They both told me how much they used to enjoy their long conversations. Lately, however, they seldom talked for more than a few minutes and then just superficially. But even that was becoming dangerous. If the conversation moved beyond superficial, they nearly always ended up in an argument without resolution. They would start by bringing up "just a little thing," but end up in a huge fight. They had become aware that their communication style was actually doing more damage to their relationship than improving it.

By the time Brett and Juli entered my office they were actually afraid to talk to each other. They had come to a point where talking meant fighting. Neither was bringing up issues or concerns; resentments were building. We worked first on the importance of listening. Juli brightened up at the idea that Brett would take time to completely hear what she wanted to say before interjecting his own thoughts and opinions. Then we discussed the importance of talking before moving on to applying conflict management skills.

After we had spent some time in sessions discussing these concepts, Brett and Juli developed their personal F.A.I.R. fighting rules. Our next session focused on bringing all those skills together to move forward toward resolution of a conflict. It was time to practice. We moved the chairs so they could sit face-to-face and knee-to-knee.

Both were understandably apprehensive about practicing in front of me, as many couples are. They had picked a topic—well, Juli had. She stated that she had an issue that had been bothering her all week and would like to bring it up here. Brett agreed, and I had them each take a minute for a few deep breaths. Juli used this time to sort out her thoughts and make them as concise as possible because she knew Brett's job would be to repeat back to her what she was about to say. After just a couple of minutes they were ready to begin. I again reminded them of the rules of listening and F.A.I.R. fighting and told them I would be guiding them gently through the steps. Juli was to start by clearly defining what the issue was so that both understood completely. This would be done by using ECHOing. Then, they would move into the resolution stage.

Juli: "I have been bothered all week by the fact that Tuesday night, when I had that terrible headache, you said you would put the dishes away after dinner so I could rest. You didn't do this."

I thought to myself, this seemed to be clear and specific enough to me. Let's see how Brett would respond.

Brett: "What I heard you say was that you were bothered that I didn't do the dishes after dinner Tuesday night like I said I would do. Is that what you meant to say?"

Well done, he seemed to hear and understand.

Juli: "No, that's not what I meant to say."

What? It sounded right to me. Did Brett and I both miss something?

Juli: "What I meant to say was that I feel you just don't do what you say you are going to do without me hounding you."

Oh, I see. Juli is upset that he isn't following through with what he says he'll do.

Brett: "What I heard you say is that you feel I don't do what I say I'm going to do and that you have to hound me to get things done. Is that what you meant to say?"

Again, it sounded to me like Brett got the meaning.

Juli: "No, that's not what I meant to say."

Man, I guess I'm really missing it, too. Usually I can tell if the spouse is getting the main points, and if not, what they are missing; not this time.

Juli: "What I meant to say was that I am frustrated that you hardly ever seem to want to help me out around the house! You are just more interested in watching TV or doing what you want to do."

Okay, I see. It was more than just a one-time thing.

Brett: "What I heard you say was that you are frustrated that I seem to be more interested in doing what I want to do than with helping you around the house. Is that what you meant to say?"

Again, I felt Brett captured what Juli had just said. Did he get it this time?

Juli: "No. That's not what I meant to say." Juli responded with a frustrated tone of voice.

They both looked at me with confusion and frustration on their faces. I encouraged them to continue. "This skill is difficult to learn, but with practice you can both begin to use it effectively. Let's just see where this is headed. Juli, why don't you continue. Clarify what it is that you are trying to say until Brett hears what you are meaning. Okay?"

"Okay." She responded hesitantly, then turned back toward Brett, took a deep breath and continued.

This process of Juli making a statement about her feelings and this particular topic and Brett repeating it back to her continued for several more minutes. From where I was sitting, Brett continued to seem accurate in his reflection. However, Juli did not seem to agree with this. Each time Brett seemed to become more and more frustrated. He would look at me with a "What am I missing?" look is his eyes and I would encourage him to keep doing what he was doing. Eventually, it all became clear.

Juli: "I guess what I'm trying to say is that I am feeling taken for granted and unappreciated by you. I feel the things I do around the house go unnoticed and that you just expect them done whether or not you help. I don't feel important to you!"

She was almost in tears by this time. The hurt was very apparent.

Brett: "What I heard you say was that you feel unappreciated and really taken for granted by me. And that you feel I don't notice all the work and time you put into our home to make it beautiful. By my not telling you that I notice and appreciate this, then you feel unimportant. Is that what you meant to say?"

Juli: "Yes! That's what I was trying to say."

And she began to cry openly. Brett took a minute to hold her. He told her he was sorry for not doing the dishes like he had agreed to, but more importantly for not letting her know how important she was to him. He openly stated his appreciation of her.

Once the real issue had been identified, the conflict resolution stage was easily handled. Juli stated her need to hear Brett's words of appreciation and asked that he follow through on the things he agrees to do.

Brett committed to telling and showing her more often how much he appreciated her taking care of their children and the home. Then he volunteered to be in charge of dinner and clean up at least one night a week. He also suggested they try to do these tasks together more often to give them some additional time together. Juli quickly agreed to these suggestions and thanked Brett for this. The conversation ended on a positive note and both Brett and Juli felt closer than they had in a long time.

We paused for a few moments to consider what had just happened, then we discussed their experience. Although they had both become frustrated during the conversation, neither one had ever used a raised voice or given up trying. I commended them for that. Then I asked them how this conversation might have occurred at home without using these new skills.

They thought a minute, then Brett responded, "I never would have understood what she was really upset about. I would probably have felt attacked at her first comment that I didn't do the dishes and that all I ever want to do is watch TV, and I probably would have started defending myself instead of listening to and hearing her." Juli was nodding as Brett continued, " I'm almost sure this would have ended up in a big fight with each of us defending and accusing and neither of us listening. As a matter of fact, we have had conversations that started like this in the past. I usually get defensive and remind Juli about all the things I do do around the house. I have been known to just get sarcastic and make hurtful comments like 'Well, I am the one with a job around here!' which always makes Juli cry and attempt to defend herself. I would get so mad that I would storm out. Man! Now that I think about it, she has probably been trying to tell me that she's felt unappreciated for a long time. And when she did, what did I do? I made her feel even more unappreciated and unimportant." Turning to Juli, he again apologized and sincerely committed to using these skills to learn to better hear and understand her.

It was through this experience that both Brett and Juli realized the value of these skills. Once a new skill has proven its effectiveness and value to you, then you will begin to focus on using it. Until then you are more likely to try it once in awhile, but not regularly and probably not effectively. I challenge you to use these new skills until they become a natural part of your communication style, and as you do they will prove their value and effectiveness to you as they have to Brett and Juli and many other couples.

# *Application*

*1. Develop your own personal "Rules for F.A.I.R. Fighting."* This chapter gave you a list of the basic rules for conflict management. These of course are important and necessary, but they don't address the specifics of you as a couple. This assignment will help you personalize a list of rules that will address the things each of you do that would be considered dirty fighting and tend to escalate a discussion into a fight.

**Step 1: The first step is to take a personal inventory of what pushes your buttons.** You know, those things your spouse can do that just send you through the roof. Maybe you were just mildly upset at first, then he or she does _____, and you are really mad and ready to fight back. These things are called your buttons or triggers, and you have to identify them if you are going to avoid them.

Let me give you an example. For me, a definite "button" is finger pointing. I mean literally. If Jim and I are having a "discussion" and he points his finger at me, I become almost instantly angry. Neither one of us actually identified this as a trigger for quite some time. We would just be disagreeing about something and then Jim might point his finger (for emphasis) while talking. Immediately I would start yelling and we would be off and running. Once we figured it out, I realized this was a long standing irritant for me. I grew up with a brother who was 18 months older than I was. And like siblings do, we often tried to aggravate each other. One of the things he did that drove me nuts was to point his finger in my face, just inches from my nose. I, of course, would yell for Mom to tell on him, to which he would respond, "I'm not touching her" (which he wasn't, not literally). I just hated that. So you can imagine how I would react when Jim showed a similar behavior. I know that may seem like a little thing, and really it is. Actually, many of our personal buttons may be little things. But if they impair our ability to communicate then we must identify them and change them if possible.

So this first step consists of making a list of "His Buttons" and "Her buttons" to identify behaviors that need to be avoided if a conflict is to reach resolution in a healthy manner. (You can use the sample form at the end of the chapter). Possible buttons may include things like: yelling, name calling, cussing, watching TV during the discussion, turning your back, walking out of the room, avoiding eye contact, comparing you to his or her mother (or your mother), or saying "Nothing" when asked "What's wrong?" These are just a few possibilities to get you thinking.

**Step 2: Once you identify your buttons, combine your lists into your personal "Rules for F.A.I.R. Fighting."** View this final list as a contract between the two of you. In other words, do not allow something to be put on the list that you know you will not be able to keep. For example, the wife in one couple I worked with identified cussing as one of her buttons. She wanted one of their rules to be "Absolutely no cussing during a conflict." Her husband openly stated that his view of what was considered "cussing" was quite different from hers. He was concerned that he would not be able to keep that rule based on her definition because he knew that he tended to use words she didn't approve of when he was angry. As they discussed this further to reach a compromise, she realized that it wasn't all cussing that triggered her, but mainly a few select words. She identified these words and her husband was able to agree to avoid those words specified on their final list.

As you write out your final list, make as many of the rules as possible in "Do" rather than "Don't" form. For example, if one of his buttons is yelling, then you might be tempted to write "Don't yell." Instead, write, "Do speak in a normal tone of voice." It's easier to comply with rules if they tell you what to do instead of what not to do. There may be some rules that you can't find a "do" way to write. When we were writing our list, we couldn't come up with a "do" way to express the finger-pointing button. We tried "Do keep you hands to your side." But we both knew that wouldn't work because I really talk with my hands. So that is one rule that stayed in the "Don't" form on our final list. The main thing is that you keep the "Don't" rules to a minimum.

As part of your final list, review the rules for F.A.I.R. fighting presented in this chapter and include the ones that seem most important to you.

**Step 3: Let's debate.** Here's your chance to practice putting the skills from the last two chapters (Listening and Talking) together on a less emotionally charged topic before you start using them in your conflicts. You may want to review the ECHO conversation and talking skills before beginning. In this assignment you will learn to listen to and ECHO back something that you very likely will disagree with. You will learn how difficult it can be to listen without interrupting and also to actually say words yourself (during the repeating phase) that don't match your personal beliefs. Once you master the skills on a more impersonal and less emotional topic, you will be more secure and ready to attempt them on an emotionally charged topic that has personal implications. Your actual rules for F.A.I.R. fighting may not come into play at this point because the topic is not personal. So focus on learning to listen (really listen, not focusing on developing your rebuttal) even when you disagree.

Find a topic on which the two of you have differing opinions but that does not directly have to do with you as a couple. In other words, pick a debate topic. If you have trouble finding a neutral topic you disagree on, you may just have to choose to take opposing views for the sake of practice. Some sample topics may include: smoking in public places; right to life topics; the best presidential candidate; the death penalty; or any other political, religious, or environmental issue.

Once you choose the topic and sides, assume the position (you know, knee-to-knee). Using the ECHOing technique, each of you present your thoughts and feelings about the topic. The listener uses the techniques from chapter 6 to encourage the speaker to continue sharing. Stay with one side until that speaker feels completely heard, and then switch roles.

The goal is not to get your spouse to agree with you or to reach any resolution regarding the topic. The goal is simply to learn to hear an opposing view and learn that "winning" is not tied to agreeing. Winning is tied to the sharing and understanding each other. This is good practice to agree to disagree, and still respect that the other person's point of view is just as valid as yours.

You may want to repeat this assignment several times over a couple of weeks in order to master the skill.

**Step 4: Evaluate an Argument.** This assignment is important to continuing to develop conflict management skills. Eventually you will have a conflict arise (for some it may be sooner than for others). Once this happens, do your best to use the skills you have learned and abide by the rules to which you have both agreed, and hopefully you will see the conflict reach resolution. But, regardless of the outcome of the conflict, at some point later (the break should be at least 30 minutes but no more than 24 hours) the two of you should sit down and evaluate how you did. Focus more on yourself than on your spouse. Look at what you did that helped as well as what you may have done that hindered. If you broke any of the rules, admit to it, apologize, and recommit to trying again. Remember, this is a learning process and will have some ups and downs. It is through this process that you will adjust and refine your rules and learn from your mistakes.

*His Buttons*

_____
_____
_____
_____
_____
_____

*Her Buttons*

_____
_____
_____
_____
_____
_____

*Our Rules for Fair Fighting*

_____
_____
_____
_____
_____
_____
_____
_____
_____
_____
_____

We agree to keep the above rules to the best of our ability and to commit ourselves to increasing our intimacy even in the midst of conflict.

_____          _____
*Signature & Date*                 *Signature & Date*

# For Your Eyes Only

## The Importance of Sexual Intimacy

*H*is left arm is under my head,
and his right arm embraces me ... .
"My lover is mine, and I am his."
*Song of Solomon 2:6, 16*

The men out there are probably saying, "Finally! I thought you would never get to the important stuff. Why is this practically at the end of the book?"

Putting this chapter earlier in the book would be like learning to swim by jumping (or being pushed) off the high dive. Most of us would fail miserably and scramble for rescue. Instead we need to learn the many components that make up swimming (breathing, treading water, floating, and strokes) and eventually graduate to the high dive. In order to graduate to a healthy sexual relationship, you will need to have first learned the components that build up to graduation, such as, warm fuzzies, good conversation skills, and F.A.I.R. fighting (just to name a few). Once these separate skills are developed, you will have a stronger sense of trust and confidence in your spouse and your marriage and the sexual part of your relationship will be easier to improve.

So many things go into building a happy, healthy marriage. Sexual intimacy is one more way to express warm fuzzies to a spouse. However, sexual intimacy is so complex that it can easily be derailed into a cold prickly if we aren't careful. The purpose of this chapter is to help you identify these complexities and better understand how to build the physical aspects of intimacy. Sexual intimacy will test your mastery of all the other skills.

You might say sexual intimacy is the Super Bowl of the relationship. Getting here proves that you have practiced hard, developed the necessary skills, and learned to work as a team. If all the necessary components were not present, you would likely have been eliminated before now. Or if you happen to make it here against all expectations, you will likely fall short of capturing the prize of true intimacy.

I think it's interesting how relationships develop (or should develop). If we follow God's plan and save sex for marriage, it's the last of many new skills we learn. If you notice, all the other skills addressed in this book can be learned, practiced, and mastered before the wedding. But sex should not be. I guess God knew what He was doing. He knew that for true sexual intimacy to develop, we must first learn to listen, talk, resolve conflicts, and touch in a non-sexual way. We must grow to a deep understanding and appreciation of each other through our verbal skills before we can really understand each other sexually. Wow! What a plan! It's just one more evidence that if we do it His way, things go much more smoothly.

## Making Love vs. Having Sex

"Is there a difference between making love and having sex?" This is a question I have posed to many couples. The responses I receive include a strong repeated nod from the wife, and a confused "Is that a trick question" look from the husband. Sometimes I phrase the question slightly differently: "Can you make love without having sex?" To which I again receive strong nods from her and even stronger confusion from him. The answer to both of these questions is, "most definitely yes."

As you will note throughout this chapter, I use the word "sex" to refer to the act of intercourse. However, I use the phrase "making love" (or physical or sexual intimacy) for just about everything else. "Making love" with your spouse is about the relationship and the emotional closeness the two of you share. It should be part of your everyday routine. It involves a combination of all the warm fuzzies that we have identified throughout this book (compliments, hugs, talking and listening, romance, etc.). It is something that you can engage in constantly if you so choose (now doesn't that sound good?). However, "sex" (intercourse) is something you look forward to and enjoy. You fit it into your daily life, but it's not a constant. It seems to fit best into the relationship when "making love" has already paved the way. We can learn to treasure our spouse through both "making love" and "having sex."

The majority of this chapter will be focused on teaching you how to make love. Only the last few pages will discuss the actual act of intercourse. (Whoa, men, don't go skipping to the end just yet. There's a lot of good stuff to learn first.)

## *Mirror, Mirror, on the Wall*

Sexual intimacy seems to be affected by almost every other aspect of your relationship, especially your communication. In most cases, the quality of your sexual relationship can be viewed as a direct reflection of the quality of communication within your marriage. For example, you may have a marriage that has developed healthy communication skills. If this is the case, both your conversations and therefore your sexual relations are more likely to be stimulating, satisfying, and deeply intimate. Each person is focused on what's best for the relationship and acts with love and respect toward the other. Our spouse's wants and needs are openly discussed and we do our best to meet those needs. We are unselfish in our interactions, and our activities are mutually agreed upon.

On the other hand, your communication may be less well developed, superficial, dull, and distant. You may view your conversations as a necessary evil, something to keep things running smoothly. The reflection of this type of communication on the physical relationship reveals sex as a duty or necessity for us each to get some needs met. We are aware of both our needs and our spouse's needs, and are willing to engage in the sexual relationship and communication, but only "as necessary." In these relationships husbands give affection to get sex and wives give sex to get affection.

Another example of how sexual intimacy reflects the quality of communication within the relationship are marriages where partners have decided that communication is just "too much trouble." In these relationships both the communication and therefore the sexual intimacy has become non-existent. These marriages have likely struggled with unhealthy patterns of communication and have reached a point of not communicating at all. When communication is nonexistent, sexual intimacy eventually disappears as well.

Finally, and the most destructive of all, is the relationship where communication has become painful, degrading, and demoralizing. These couples communicate, but mainly in harmful patterns. Their conversations are almost always confrontational and cutting. They focus on getting their needs met at any cost, having their say, and belittling their spouse. They actually seem to want to hurt each other. Their sexual relationship lacks respect for the other's wants or needs. Requests from their spouse to do or not do particular things are often ignored completely, and personal needs and wants are put as the first (and only) priority. As you can guess, these relationships are destructive and in need of immediate intervention by a professional.

As you work to improve the sexual dimension of your marriage, be sure to evaluate and improve, if necessary, the quality of your communication. As your communication skills become stronger and healthier, so will the reflection.

## *Where Did All the Passion Go?*

When I met Joe and Kathy, they had been married three years. They were nervous and exceptionally quiet entering my office. As they fidgeted on the couch, I asked them to describe for me why they were there. The fidgeting increased as each looked at the other expectantly, as if to say, "go ahead, you start." The silence lasted for what seemed to me like minutes (I'm sure it seemed more like years to each of them) before Joe blurted out "We never have sex anymore." To which Kathy quickly responded, "That's not true. It's just that seems to be all he ever wants to do." And with just those two statements I knew where we were headed.

As I gathered the history of their relationship, I learned that they had met and dated through college and had truly enjoyed their dating experiences. They seemed to have done everything right. Their relationship had developed slowly. They became friends through a Bible study group where they often found themselves hanging around for hours afterwards just talking. As their friendship grew they found they had several things in common. They began spending time together outside the Bible study and before long they seemed inseparable. They studied together, went on long walks holding hands, talked endlessly, and kissed tenderly.

Kathy reported feeling like she was the most important thing in the world to Joe. He treated her like a lady. He opened doors for her, held her chair at restaurants (even Burger King®), helped her with her coat, and often carried her books. She hadn't realized such men still existed, but she was glad she had found one. He was also a natural romantic (or so she thought at the time). He planned romantic dinners, seemed to enjoy romantic movies, and wrote her love notes with poems he'd made up himself (they were a little corny at times, but she loved the effort).

What made the biggest impact on her, though, was his commitment to abstaining from sex until after marriage. Now she knew she had an endangered species standing before her and she wanted to hang on to him forever. This decision made him all the more attractive to her. It allowed her to relax and enjoy the dating experience to its fullest extent, without worry about having to beat him off with a stick by the end of the evening (like she had done with so many other guys she had dated).

As their relationship progressed, marriage bells began to ring. They were both excited about the prospect of spending the rest of their lives with their best friend. The late night talks continued and often ended with a time of holding each other and kissing passionately. They kept to their commitment of abstinence, but they both were aware of how difficult this was becoming as the wedding drew nearer. They often talked about what sex would be like and how they couldn't wait for the honeymoon.

The wedding finally arrived, as did the wedding night (which they both enjoyed, but also admitted was not all what they had hoped it would be).They were both exhausted by the time they reached their hotel and their first sexual encounter seemed to be more out of obligation and expectation than anything else. Although at the time neither one talked about it, they were both disappointed. Luckily, things did improve from there (at least for a little while). Once they were rested, things began to fall more into place with their separate (but never discussed) expectations of their sexual intimacy.

Over the next several months, Joe and Kathy both reported feeling fairly satisfied with their life together, particularly the development of their physical intimacy. But before long, Kathy noticed that Joe wasn't as interested in their walks together or holding hands while they were riding in the car, and he seldom remembered to open the door for her. She had known that some things would change after marriage so she let much of this pass without saying a word about how she missed those little affections. But that wasn't all that changed. Things between them just continued to fizzle as far as she was concerned. She began to notice that every time they began to cuddle, hug, or kiss (even the little kisses), Joe seemed to become aroused immediately. These little acts of affection seemed to always turn into foreplay and before she knew it they would end up in the bedroom (or any other place in the house). "That" seemed to be all he ever wanted anymore. What happened to her endangered species? Had she only been fooling herself? Was he really like all those other men, only interested in one thing? As her disappointments grew, she found herself pulling away from him whenever he touched her. He would say, "Hey, I just wanted to hug you." And she would think to herself, *Yeah right, I've heard that before.* It wasn't long before they weren't engaging in any physical contact for days or sometimes weeks at a time. She knew something was wrong. Was it her? Him? Them?

Next I asked Joe to share his experience with me. He agreed with much of how Kathy had described their relationship, and then went on to share his frustrations with the relationship as it stood at that time. He expressed that he felt he had won the best prize ever when he married Kathy. She was beautiful and exciting to be around. She shared many of his recreational interests and loved God with all her heart. What more could he ask for—other than sex, which he did often. After all, they were newlyweds. Weren't they supposed to spend the first year of their marriage in bed? Or at least the first few months? They had waited so long to fulfill this part of their relationship and he was excited about it all the time.

Before they married, Joe had fantasized about how wonderful their sex life would be. He was sure Kathy was just as excited about it as he was because before the wedding they had talked about it often. And he knew how difficult it had become for both of them to stop during those last few months before the wedding. She was getting just as aroused as he was. Now they didn't have to wait anymore, and he couldn't seem to keep his hands off of her (especially those previously "forbidden" zones). But before long, it seemed that he couldn't get her interested. She would just pull away and say, "Not now, honey," or "not here." What do you mean "not now"? To him there was no better time than right now and no better place than right here. Wasn't this supposed to be the best part of their marriage? Where sex is spontaneous and creative, where "anything goes" before the humdrum of married life sets in? If this is the "best," he wasn't sure he wanted to see what "humdrum" would be like.

Joe expressed missing the long passionate kisses they used to experience. "Now she hardly let's me kiss her on the cheek before I leave for work." He missed hugging and holding her body close to his. "Now she seems to shudder a little when I come up behind her and put my arms around her waist. I'm just wanting to hold her, but she pulls away." As he shared his frustrations, it was evident he was hurting. He began to ask the question "why?" "Doesn't she want this as much as I do? Is there something wrong with me? Her? Us?"

I assured each of them that there was nothing "wrong" with them. They were experiencing a very common problem in marital relationships and that they weren't telling me anything I hadn't heard before. Over the course of the next few months, I shared with Joe and Kathy much of what I have presented in this book so far. They had to learn to get things in the right order, to reprioritize the various aspects of their relationship. They had to wait until toward the end of therapy (like you have had to wait until the end of this book) to actually talk about what they thought they had come in for, "sex." And even then (like this chapter), they had to learn other aspects of making love before we discussed "the act."

Joe and Kathy, like most couples, learned that when the other aspects of the relationship are on track, then the physical part will proceed full steam ahead. By the time we were ready to actually discuss sex in session, both of them reported already having seen improvements in that area. And over time they saw their relationship blossom and grow.

Even after having learned many of the other skills necessary for the developing of healthy sexual intimacy, Joe and Kathy needed to spend time learning how their differences could either strengthen or threaten their marriage.

## *What's the Diff?*

The differences between men and women are talked about everywhere and are evident in every area of our lives. But nowhere are these differences more obvious than in the bedroom. There seem to be practically no similarities—except maybe that we are both absolutely confused by the other's views, responses, and needs when it comes to sex. These differences are discussed in just about every book you pick up on marriage. The table below and the discussion of differences that follows were adapted from several great authors on the topic[1] (with a few additions of my own).

**Differences between Men and Women:**
Affection is …
Him: Foreplay
Her: Closeness

Foreplay is …
Him: A means to an end; something to be endured
Her: The best part of the act; something to be treasured
Biggest "turn on" is …
Him: Her naked body
Her: Conversation
Post play refers to …
Him: Rolling over to catch my breath
Her: Cuddling and talking
Arousal is …
Him: Spontaneous
Her: A choice
Oneness is …
Him: Physical
Her: Emotional
Priority of "the act" is …
Him: Very high
Her: Middle to low
During "the act" …
Him: Difficult to distract
Her: Easily distracted
Role (usually) is …
Him: Initiator
Her: Responder
Timing is …
Him: Anytime, Anywhere
Her: When it feels right
Sees events of the day as …
Him: Separate
Her: Connected
Desire begins in the …
Him: Eyes or imagination
Her: Mind or touch
Arousal and climax are …
Him: Rapid
Her: Gradual

Do we have anything in common? Not much — mainly our confusion and frustration. But don't lose hope. Where there's a will there's a way. And believe me, sexual intimacy is worth fighting for.

# *Sex: One of His Essentials for Life*

Let's look at a man's core make up as it relates sex. Sexual activity for a man can be likened to his view of money. He absolutely loves it. He is willing to work for it (usually), but prefers it to come easily. He seems to never have enough of it. Even if he were to receive a large "bonus" today, he would very much like to have another one tomorrow and the next day and the next day. He can never seem to get enough to totally satisfy his desire. It is what his world revolves around and he truly believes he cannot live without it.

This is really not far from the truth for most men. They are sexual beings through and through. Husbands think about sex more often than their wives, are aroused much more quickly and spontaneously, and place a much higher priority on the act of sex . They are aroused visually by our bodies (even when women feel anything but sexy), and acts of affection are really defined as foreplay in their minds.

His ability to separate events in his mind makes it possible for him to be "in the mood" anytime and anywhere (even if you just had a two-hour argument over how his mother's meatloaf is better than yours is). His mind seems one-tracked when it comes to sex. He doesn't consider what happened moments before or what will happen later. He also doesn't consider what else might be going on at the same time. He is difficult to distract. The fact that the kids are awake and running around the house unsupervised means very little once he has zoned in on his target.

Now don't get me wrong. This creature I just described is not some kind of an animal (although he may act like it at times); he's your husband. He is not a force to be reckoned with or a beast to be tamed. He is the man that you love, and making love to you is essential to his life and how he views himself and the marriage.

A loving wife needs to identify the differences between her and her husband and evaluate how best to meet his needs. If we truly understand that sex is a need for our husbands, we will be more willing and able to move toward meeting that need. For men, sex really is more than a recreational activity. His sexual performance is tied directly to his self-image. Experiencing a healthy sexual relationship builds his confidence as a man and husband. Without this, his feelings of insecurity may grow and he may find himself looking elsewhere for this type of affirmation. Not meeting this need could place a weak link in your marriage. Meeting our husband's sexual needs not only makes him feel more secure as a man, it also protects the security of our marriage.

## Affection: The Air That She Breathes

Okay, men, now it's your turn. How can you ever understand this creature called woman? Why is she so different from you? Was this God's little joke? Create man with an insatiable need for something that his partner seems to never want? No, I don't think so.

Let's look at it this way: for women, sex is much like having a nice, rich piece of chocolate cake. It is one of those little luxuries of life that we allow ourselves to indulge in periodically. It seems to fit best at the end of a full course meal of conversation, affection, and various other warm fuzzies. It is a perfect ending to a perfect meal. As a matter of fact, we like to take our time with this experience, to savor every bite, and truly enjoy its rich and satisfying nature. And once we have indulged, we are satisfied for a while. We usually don't want another piece right away or maybe even for several days. We are content to savor the memory of the last piece of cake and how wonderful it was.

Get the picture? It's not that she doesn't enjoy sex, because most women do. It's simply that she doesn't require it the way you do. For her, the cake is the foreplay and intercourse is the "icing" (so to speak) of the relationship. Icing isn't much good without the cake to put it on. On the other hand, even cake without icing is often very enjoyable. So how do you get to the "icing"? Take time to fix the full course meal and bake the cake, then I'm sure she will be more than happy to ice it for you.

Men, your wife is turned on not by your naked body as much as by your conversation. She is aroused by the affection (nonsexual touch and acts of kindness) that you show her throughout the day. For her, arousal is a choice and is most likely a result of the events of the past several hours or days, not just the here and now. She is likely to initiate less often than you would like and then, only when the timing is "right." Arousal and climax for her is a gradual process, and she can become easily distracted during the process.

The key concept for women is affection. The presence of affection is absolutely essential for her to experience a satisfying sexual relationship. Affection refers to acts of kindness and love. These acts are not sexual in nature. Rather, they are given solely for the purpose of expressing caring and closeness. Acts of affection include things like holding hands, hugs, cards, flowers, notes left to be found later, winks, opening doors, and many more. Physical affection is shown through nonsexual ("safe") touch. In her mind, affection symbolizes those things she needs most. These include security, comfort, approval, bonding, and protection. The simple act of giving a hug to her can say so much. Acts of affection such as hugs say, "I love you," "I'm proud of you," "I think you're wonderful," or "I'm sorry you're hurting." All of these make up the air that she breathes and are essential to the life of her marriage. If affection is absent, women feel insecure, distant, and unloved, and the marriage is at risk. When an essential element of the relationship is missing, the marriage weakens and is exposed to the threat of looking outside the marriage to get what's missing.

## *"How Am I Doing, Coach?"*

Although the differences between men and women can pose great threats to our marriages, this does not have to be the case. There is no need to be afraid of these differences. Through our differences we are given the chance to learn more about our spouse and grow to a greater level of intimacy. When I meet with couples to work on improving their sexual relations, I hear two major complaints. From men I hear, "There is not enough sex." From women I hear, "There is not enough affection." Not surprising, based on what we now know about the differences between men and women. As I meet with these couples, I tell them that they each hold the key to meeting the other's most vital need. She holds the key to meeting his sexual need, and he holds the key to meeting her affection need. I then often hear something like, "I'm not the affectionate type" or "I don't know what pleases him sexually." Okay, then it's time to learn.

How do you learn? How would you go about learning anything that's really important to you? Go to an expert in the field, either personally, through a class, or maybe a book. For example, if you wanted to learn to play tennis, you would probably find an expert at the game to coach you. You would listen carefully to instruction and then do your best to follow directions. You would practice the skills and allow your coach to help you refine your game. You would be open to feedback. This would take some time.

If the skill you want to learn is to meet your spouse's vital needs in the area of sexual intimacy, then identify the expert in this field. This, of course, is none other than your spouse. Learning to meet his or her vital needs means asking for instruction. Openly ask to be coached, and be willing to accept the suggestions given.

The coach, in return, should openly agree to teach in an encouraging manner. I doubt you would continue with your tennis coach if all he did was tell you what you did wrong and how you are never going to get it right. If the coach is belittling, you will quickly lose interest in the game. So as coach, be careful not to discourage the efforts your spouse is making. Give plenty of positive reinforcement and encouragement to keep your student interested and improving. Be willing to get very specific.

One note of warning: It doesn't mean less just because it didn't come naturally. Often people, women especially, believe that it doesn't mean as much if I have to ask for it (or have to teach it). Even the most naturally talented tennis player out there had to take lessons, learn skills, practice regularly before the actions became spontaneous. "Spontaneous" doesn't happen until the skills are well learned. No tennis player who wins Wimbledon thinks it means less because he or she had to take lessons. Be patient and continue coaching; enjoy the learning process. Remember that you are each very different in your needs, so what comes naturally to you will most likely not be what your spouse needs. If you will take time to learn about and understand these differences, you will be one step closer to sexual fulfillment.

You may wonder at times if all this emphasis on our differences is really necessary. Are we really that different? Do these difference really affect the way we interact with our spouse? Let me give you a real-life example from my own marriage that shows how obvious these differences can be and how real the impact was for us.

## Real Life

While I was in the process of writing this book, Jim planned a weekend away for me to just focus on writing. This was a huge warm fuzzy for me, and I made sure he knew how much I appreciated it. After two days away, I was exhausted from very little sleep. I was returning to my family after what seemed like an eternity of practically no human contact (other than strangers in the hotel lobby and the maid) and no talking (except to myself and when I was really desperate, to my laptop). The few brief phone contacts with Jim and the kids were nice, but not enough for me. I couldn't wait to get home and reconnect with my family through conversations and hugs.

Jim, on the other hand, had spent the last couple of days entertaining and wrestling with our three kids. He missed his wife. He had dreamed about being at the hotel with her and truly wished he were. His natural, male tendencies made him look forward to seeing and touching her. After all, what better way to reconnect than to have sex?

You can probably see where this is heading, but before I go a step further, let me remind you that neither of us was "wrong" in our hopes and desires. We were both just very different (naturally different). But it was these natural difference that caused the problem.

To continue: I came home to an empty house (everyone was at church), and vegged out while I waited for my family's return. I was tired of being alone. I found myself fantasizing about those first smiles and hugs.

The kids were first to file in, and I was quickly met with their gleeful squeals of "Yeah! Mama's home!" and great big hugs. I was feeling better already. By the time Jim made it in the house (arms full of coloring pages, diaper bag, and Bibles), I had one child on each leg and one in my arms and wrapped around my neck. I see a glimpse of disappointment (or maybe it was a look of "what's left for me") in his eyes as he playfully walks right by me and pretends to hug thin air. Our first contact was a five-person hug, which I loved, but probably didn't do much for him. He had been hugging them all weekend. What he really wanted and needed was to get hold of me. Even the hug that he got after I was able to shed at least two of the three kids was not exactly what he wanted. I needed to reconnect with the whole family. Jim had connected with the kids all weekend through quality daddy time. What he needed was to connect with me. We both had different needs as well as different expectations.

As we went through the motions of daily life (fixing lunch, changing diapers, cleaning up), we were each looking for the other to be open and understanding of what "I" needed. I was talking non-stop (or whenever the kids weren't) and wanted him to talk to me about his weekend as well, which he was doing, but in smaller bits and chunks than I wanted. During these conversations, he was throwing in sexual comments and touching (maybe a better word would be groping) whenever I was within reach. There was absolutely nothing wrong or inappropriate about his touch; however, I was not so appropriate in my response. I wasn't ready yet to be touched in that way. My exhaustion was evident as I let him know, in no uncertain terms, that I didn't appreciate being "manhandled." Why couldn't he just hold me and talk to me? Was that too much to ask? He was surprised at my reaction, and responded with telling me he had been talking to me and did hug me when I got home, and that he hadn't been "groping," he had just missed me. This was followed by a sarcastic "Sorrrrrry." And throwing his hands up in the air.

I won't bore you with the rest of the details; suffice it to say we both did more hurting each other than reconnecting for the next 20 or 30 minutes. Eventually we went to our separate corners to cool off. That's when it hit me. I had been working on this very chapter while I was away for the weekend (guess I hadn't been listening too well when I was talking to myself). I had just finished writing about the differences between men and women. You would think I should have been able to predict how different our needs would have been after a few days apart. But, obviously I didn't. All I thought about was what I needed, and at some level I'm sure that's what Jim did also. It was humorous to me at this point, and so obvious. I was able to go to Jim and share with him what I thought had just happened. He wasn't quite as amused as I was, but we were both able to forgive and move past this. We worked hard to reconnect, and I am happy to say, the rest of the evening went much better.

Now that we have worked on understanding our different physical needs and the importance of making love all through the day, let me give you some practical suggestions to improve the act of sex.

## How to Improve Your Sexual Relationship

*1. Make it a priority.* Amid our busy schedules and constant responsibilities, it is easy to lose track of the need to connect physically. Remember the importance of sexual intimacy in your relationship and be willing to make time for it. Don't hesitate to pencil in private time with your spouse on your calendar or take a weekend away to a hotel for privacy.

*2. Slow down.* I have heard a good friend of mine, Gary Smalley, say that in the world of sex, men are microwave ovens and women are crock pots. What a picture! For women, the meal of physical intimacy is all day in the preparing. Making love to her begins with a tender kiss to wake her, winking at her from over your first cup of coffee, and calling her from work to tell her you miss her. Then it continues through helping her with dinner and getting the kids to bed, and taking time to snuggle during your favorite TV program. Once in bed you take time to touch, touch, and touch some more. Foreplay is an end in itself. Her skin is one of her most powerful sexual organs; caress it often. Although this may not be a husband's natural tendency, he will quickly learn that he enjoys the slow-cooked meal more than the microwave kind and will choose it often.

*3. Set the stage.* Never forget the power of clean sheets, a candlelit room, and soft music. Remember, making love is much more than the act of intercourse. Create a quiet, slow, soft, and relaxed environment, and your internal mood begins to match that. You will be better able to push aside the outside world and stress of the day and slow down and enjoy your time together.

*4. Talk before, during, and after.* She probably can't get enough of this. The more you talk, the more she will respond, because she feels closer and more connected to you through talking. Share with each other what you like and what you don't like. Whisper sweet, romantic words as you make love. Let her know she's important to you and all you are thinking about. Let him know that he pleases you.

*5. Take care of yourself physically.* Do your best to look your best. This means more than just staying in shape, or losing that extra 10 or 20 pounds. Take time to dress nicely even if you are just staying home for the evening. Wives, get out of those old sweats with the hole in the seat that you would never be caught dead in out in public and that you have had on all day while you cleaned toilets and scrubbed floors. Take a shower and freshen up. Do your hair and make up, and get rid of those ponytails and bobby pins.

Husbands, remove those old work jeans covered with dirt and oil from the last four times you wore them (and put them somewhere other than draped over the bed). Shower and shave, clip you fingernails and put on something other than your favorite pair of boxers. Both of you will feel better and be more responsive to being touched.

Don't get me wrong, there is a time and place for those old scrubbies at home. Just don't let that side of you be all he or she sees.

*6. Get involved.* Women, learn to be more than a recipient. He will love it when you initiate sexual activity. Do so aggressively and creatively. Make yourself "sexy." Remember, he's very visual so plan that evening alone and put on some lingerie, or surprise him at the door with only an apron on and watch his reaction.

*7. Be creative and spontaneous.* This applies to both time and activity. Avoid getting stuck in a sexual rut. I met one couple who had sex once a week (and only once) on Saturday morning. They practically set their watches to it. Now don't get me wrong, there is nothing wrong with having set-aside time for intimacy. But don't get rigid about this. Focus on variety in time of day, place, position, setting, etc. Keep it interesting and exciting.

*8. Invest in your relationship.* We spend money on just about anything and everything and then say we can't afford a weekend away or dinner out with our spouse. Bite the bullet, get a baby-sitter, and go for it. The dividends are tremendous.

*9. Be honest.* With both your mouth and your body. Communication in any and all forms should be honest. Sex is a form of physical communication. Commit yourselves honestly with your body. Don't fake interest, arousal, enjoyment, or orgasm. If you aren't in the mood, or if something doesn't feel comfortable, talk about it. Dishonesty in the bedroom is just as destructive to the foundation of your relationship as lying with words.

*10. Focus more on giving than receiving.* A major threat to developing a strong, healthy sexual relationship is selfishness. Be aware of what your spouse needs or wants and focus on giving that. Pay attention to moods and energy levels. Avoid the trap of "I will do what you ask as soon as you do what I ask." This usually ends up with neither of you getting your needs met. Instead, focus on being the first one to meet the other's needs. If you both have this attitude, you will both end up getting your needs met.

## *Application*

Several exercises will help you better understand what your spouse needs and how to improve physical intimacy. These include improving your ability to talk about your needs and wants, and learning to make love without having sex.

*1. Discussion Time.* One of the best ways to improve your sexual relationship is to learn to openly share what you like and dislike. For many couples, this is a difficult topic of discussion. But, if you remember and use your ECHOing skills as well as Conversation Nourishers from earlier chapters, you should be able to handle this discussion well.

To begin, separately take time to think about and complete the statements listed below. These will help you in starting the conversation as well as in thinking through your own personal needs and desires. These will also help in keeping the conversation on track. Feel free to add statements of your own. Once you have completed the questions, set a time to discuss these knee-to-knee. Be open in your descriptions, and if you don't understand completely what your spouse is saying, be sure to ask.

I feel satisfied when you …
I don't enjoy it when you …
I wish you would …
A sexual need or desire I have that you may not be aware of is …

2. *Touch Exercise.* This is one of the most important keys to learning to make love without having intercourse. This exercise works best with a commitment between the two of you to have no intercourse for two weeks. I know that may seem like forever for some of you (and maybe no big deal for others), but I think you will understand the benefits as I describe the exercise. If you feel you cannot make the "no intercourse" commitment, then at least commit to no intercourse during, or immediately after, this exercise.

The purpose of this exercise is two fold: (1) to teach men the importance and enjoyment of touch for touch sake only, and not as a means to an end. (2) To help women begin again to give and accept touch without pulling away. As I mentioned earlier in the chapter, many women are not only pulling away from their husband's touch, but also not reaching out themselves to touch their husbands because of the experience that touch leads to sex. The commitment of "no intercourse" will help her feel more secure and more willing to open up and truly enjoy this exercise. Husbands, if you make the commitment for two weeks, you will notice her accepting and giving more "safe" touch than you might have imagined possible. And I'm almost sure those passionate kisses and long full-body hugs will return.

The exercise itself should take approximately 30 minutes each time. One of you will be the giver and one the receiver. Don't both try to be the receiver in the same evening. The receiver will be totally relaxed by the end of the exercise, and the last thing you will want to do is get up and give to the other one. So let the receiver relax and in the next night or two do it again with roles reversed. The exercise is also best done with the receiver nude. If this is too uncomfortable for either of you, make the minimal adjustments necessary to be more comfortable.

So what is the exercise? The giver is to touch the receiver from head to toe (excluding genital areas) in every way imaginable with his or her hands. Explore several different types of touch you can do with your hands including fingertip tickle, fingernail tickle, tips of fingers massage, heel of hand massage, and full hand touch. You may even come up with some more. Use as many different types of touch on as many different parts of the body as possible. Use common sense and wisdom as you touch. For instance, you would not do a deep heel of the hand massage on the face, but you could do several other types. Also be aware of ticklish zones. Some people may be ticklish from head to toe. For them, there are likely certain places on their body to which they absolutely could not handle a fingernail tickle. But those same places may be able to accept a full hand rub or deeper massage. Be very considerate and in tune to how your spouse responds to your different touches.

The job of the receiver is first of all, to enjoy, enjoy, enjoy; and secondly, to give feedback to your spouse about what you like and what you don't like. Tell your spouse which types of touches are:

• relaxing ("I would like that type of touch after a rough day at work.")
• stimulating ("I really like that, but you had better stop for now if we are going to keep our commitment.")
• uncomfortable ("I'd rather you not do that there, it doesn't feel comfortable.")

After you have each been the receiver a couple of times, you may (with each other's permission) adjust the exercise to include genital areas. Remember, the "no intercourse" commitment still stands. Learn to pleasure each other in other ways.

3. *Touch Game.* This is a variation of the touch exercise that adds a little more fun and games to the bedroom. In this variation, each of you collects five objects from around the house and places them in a brown paper bag. These should be of different textures, temperatures, sizes, etc. You will then take turns touching each other's bodies with these objects. You may choose to blindfold (no peeking) the receiver or only touch on the back of the body. The receiver's job is to guess the object. The one with the most correct guesses is the winner. I will leave the prize up to the two of you!

This can be a fun and playful competition for the two of you. But don't try to get tricky. I had one couple come in after having been given this assignment. The husband proudly announced that he had "won" to which his wife stated, "you cheated." As they described the game, I found out that he had touched her with a circular metal object (about one inch in diameter). She had guessed a quarter or other coin and a couple other things, all of which were wrong. When I asked what the mystery object was. He proudly announced, "a hammer." Everyone got a good laugh out of it, and she committed to getting trickier the next time they played. So a note of fairness: be sure to give your spouse enough information about the object to formulate an educated guess. But most of all have fun.

*4. Add Some Spice.* This exercise is to help you avoid slipping into a rut in your sexual lives. All too often married couples fall into the rut of same place, same time or same position, as it relates to making love. I encourage you to avoid this rut at all cost. Allow yourselves to be spontaneous and creative whenever possible. Use the list at the end of this chapter to give you some ideas of how to spice up your sex life. Read the list together and discuss which of these suggestions you may or may not be comfortable trying (not everything is for everyone). Then be sure to add a few of your own ideas. And whenever possible, start trying them.

# Suggestions for Spicing Up Your Sex Life

1. Give each other body massages with your favorite scent of lotion or oil.
2. Share a fantasy.
3. Act out a fantasy.
4. Play the Touch Game.
5. Be a human banana split.
6. Play a romantic or erotic board game.
7. Give each other a shower.
8. Take a bubble bath together.
9. Go parking—get in the back seat!
10. Undress slowly for each other.
11. Make love without intercourse.
12. Wear sexy lingerie.
13. Make love in unusual places.
14. Put a lock on your door—and don't be afraid to use it.
15. Dance or strip for each other.
16. Be risky.
17. Ask your spouse what he or she likes and do it.
18. Take turns being "in control" (leading).
19. Grab a "quickie" in the middle of the day.
20. Touch frequently and lovingly throughout the day.
21. Take time to kiss—really kiss.
22. Make love in every room of the house (and beyond).
23. Call your spouse at work and talk dirty to them (if allowed).

24. Play strip poker (or any game; Strip Go Fish will do).
25. Meet your spouse at the door after work dressed in only a tie or apron.
26. Send a note in your spouse's lunch alluding to exciting events planned for the evening.
27. Try new positions.
28. Kidnap your spouse from work and head to hotel.
29. Try a vibrator.
30. Play your favorite love songs in the background.

# 9

# *This Isn't What I Expected!*

The Power of Expectations and Priorities

T urn my eyes away from worthless things."
*Psalm 119:37*

"And they lived happily ever after."

As I finished reading Tiara one of her favorite fairy tales, I wondered, what is this teaching her? I remember daydreaming about having a fairy godmother who could make me beautiful, finding Prince Charming, and being whisked away to live "happily ever after." None of this actually happened in my life (well, except finding Prince Charming). I never received a magical makeover or a wardrobe full of ball gowns and glass slippers. I certainly didn't get whisked away to a castle (as a matter of fact, our first house was so small we called it the "baby house"), and life together has not exactly always been my idea of "happily ever after."

Do you think Cinderella and Prince Charming's carriage ever hit bumps in the road? Did they disagree about how to arrange the furniture? Was the lid of the toothpaste tube or the toilet seat the topic of long, heated discussions? Did Cinderella ever feel neglected when he was gone for days fighting dragons? Were their different backgrounds ever a source of contention?

Each of us enters our relationship with a set of preconceived expectations. Whether conscious or unconscious, they have been a long time in the making. Our expectations of marriage begin to form in very early life. As small children, we read stories, watch movies, and observe our parents, family, and friends. Each of these gives us a part of what grows to be our personal expectations of what marriage will be like. Since each of us has different experiences growing up, we each develop different expectations. And even if you could find that perfect someone who has had exactly the same background as you, your perceptions still would not match, because the person you are married to is of the opposite sex. I have met very few men who look back over their childhood and remember daydreaming about meeting Cinderella, or dressing up Barbie and Ken and playing wedding. (The only time I remember my brother showing any interest in Barbie was when GI Joe needed something for target practice.)

## Stages of Marriage

As we travel down the yellow brick road in search of the fairy tale marriage, we encounter three distinctly differently lands. What we learn about ourselves and our spouse through each of these experiences can teach us what we need to know to reach the prize of a healthy, life-long, satisfying relationship.

The first land we encounter is the Land of Rose-Colored Glasses. This is an enchanting place filled with beauty and treasures. As we enter we are handed a pair of rose-colored glasses. These glasses make us see the world in a brand new way. The gleaming pink color overlaid on everything we see transforms even slightly ugly creatures or flowers to things of beauty.

Couples start their travels here. This is the honeymoon and early marriage stage. Couples remain in the Land of Rose-Colored Glasses anywhere from hours, weeks, months, or for the very lucky, years. In this stage we truly believe we have already reached the Land of "Happily Ever After." Of course we have seen the devastation and break-ups of relationships around us, but that won't (can't) happen to us. After all, we're in love and we are perfect for each other. Nothing could possibly come between us. No problem is insurmountable. We know what we want out of life and marriage. We probably haven't talked about this, but really there's no need to because we always think alike (or at least that's what we tell ourselves in this land). This land is often filled with assumptions and unstated expectations and rules. We don't take time to talk through our rules, goals, and expectations because we "just know" (assume) that our spouse is thinking just like we are. After all, "I know you are

perfect because you are just like me." This is the time of open dis-
plays of romance, of long, late-night talks, and of overlooking those
little irritants (after all, he is kind of cute when he does that). Warm
fuzzies fill our vision everywhere we look.

Regardless of how long this stage lasts, it is important in building
the foundation of a life-long relationship. During this stage we learn
that we can enjoy each other. We depend on each other and we feel
loved, nurtured, and satisfied. This should be a mutually enjoyable
and satisfying time in your relationship—one that many of us will
look back on fondly. But in order to reach our final destination, we
must at some point leave this land and venture on.

The next land we encounter is the Disenchanting Forest. We usually enter this land immediately upon removing our rose-colored
glasses. Although not nearly as enjoyable as the honeymoon stage,
this stage is also normal and necessary for the development of a life-
long marriage. Reality sets in. Prince Charming's shining armor is
dented and smudged. Cinderella's crown is tarnished and crooked
(or maybe has fallen completely off).

In the disillusionment stage, we begin to see our spouses as real
persons with real faults. They fall off their pedestals, and sometimes
this fall really hurts. For many marriages today, this is the beginning
of the end. We say, "you aren't living up to the promises you made,"
although many of these "promises" were assumed rather than made.
Rules that had gone unspoken in the honeymoon stage (because we
were sure we each knew the rules) are now spoken (and very loud-
ly I might add) because they have been broken.

As couples realize that their spouses cannot meet their every need
(and probably don't want to), all too many head directly to the attorney's office to divorce and start over on their search for Prince
Charming or Cinderella. In our society of "satisfaction guaranteed or
your money back," the disillusionment stage can become the kiss of
death to many marriages. All of a sudden we are not satisfied and we
want to return him or her for a full refund. Unfortunately, this more
costly than we may ever know.

In this stage we begin to see the gap between our expectations of
marriage and the reality of two very different people working to
blend into one. We are rudely awakened early Saturday morning by
our spouse whistling while she vacuums right beside the bed.
Doesn't she know Saturdays are for sleeping in and lounging around
most of the morning? Or maybe it's his dirty clothes lying beside the
clothes hamper instead of in it. Maybe it's the first really big fight.
"He actually yelled at me! How could he! He's never talked like that

to me before." Or try this one, "I can't believe she expects me to clean up the kitchen just because she cooked dinner. Why can't she do it? My mom always took care of those kinds of things."

Warm fuzzies begin to decline and we move to a focus on cold pricklies. This is the stage of "He or she used to …" This stage is unavoidable. Through the closeness of the honeymoon stage, we really get to know each other. As we open our hearts, we learn both the good and the bad about each other. And the more we learn, the less perfect he or she looks. Although this stage is unavoidable, we don't have to fear it. With the proper understanding and good communication skills, you can weather this storm and reach the sunny skies on the other side.

The third land is the Land of Happily Ever After. If we have had the strength and love necessary to survive the Disenchanting Forest, our efforts will be rewarded. As we forged through the forest, we learned the skills of acceptance and adjustment and proved ourselves honorable and worthy of reaching the final Land of Happily Ever After. Here is where we find fulfillment. Many of us thought that Happily Ever After began at the end of the wedding ceremony; that is not the case. As the wedding ends, the journey begins. The journey may take years and won't be without its hills and valleys, but the persistent will reach the Land of Happily Ever After.

This is the stage of accommodation, adjustment, and acceptance. How do we move from disillusionment to fulfillment? First, we must identify our expectations. Remember those unspoken rules of the honeymoon stage, which we find in the disillusionment stage have been broken? Learn to identify what these are, speak them out loud, and evaluate how realistic they really are. If the expectations are realistic, all that may be necessary is bringing them out into the open. However, many of our expectations are not realistic and therefore will need to be adjusted. In order to develop a more realistic set of expectations for your marriage, you will need to use your ECHO conversation skills (chapter 5). As you discuss these together, you will begin to set new expectations that you are both aware of and agree to.

Holding onto unrealistic expectations can cause us unnecessary heartache. Let's take some time to understand where expectations come from, why they often go unmet; and then let's identify a few of the commonly held unrealistic ones.

# *Where Do We Get Expectations?*

Expectations for marriage begin to develop from very early childhood. We develop our perceptions of what life together will be like from watching our parents or other adults in our lives. Our perceived happiness, satisfaction, and contentment are all based on our expectations. Whether we feel satisfied in our marriage depends on what we expected it would be like, and how close reality is to that expectation. Let me take a personal example here. I had spent several months working on the manuscript of this book and was making only slow progress. I could rationally look at my life and understand why. I was carrying a full caseload of clients at our counseling center as well as supervising several therapists and their caseloads. I was also involved with the administration of the company (when I could find the time to help Jim out). Time away from work was filled with the joys and trials of three young children, attempting to buy and sell a home and finding time for Jim. (Unfortunately he often got the crumbs. Maybe I better read the "How to T.R.E.A.S.U.R.E." section again.) You get the picture. Life was already busy, and I added writing a book on top of it all. Not only did I decide to write a book, but I expected it to take just a few months to accomplish. Ha! What was I thinking? Perhaps, if I had locked myself up in a padded room (which, believe me, has been considered, probably more by Jim than by me) for a few months, then maybe, and that's a big "maybe," I could have gotten it done.

As the months wore on and my expectations didn't change, my frustrations grew. Finally, for the sanity of my family and myself, I relaxed a little, realizing that I needed to slow down and not pressure myself so much. After all, it's not like I was on some kind of deadline or anything. I didn't have a publisher breathing down my back yet. (Actually, at this point I wasn't completely sure I would ever have a publisher.) I had been doing this to myself. What was I thinking? Slow down, take it easy, enjoy life, get your priorities back on track, Debbie. It was just about at the "take it easy" part that things changed again. A publisher showed interest, as did a wonderfully encouraging man named Gary Smalley, and things were off and running again. I moved from the expectations I had placed on myself, to expectations being placed on me from outside sources, called deadlines. And with the deadlines quickly approaching, I began to panic. How in the world was I going to get this book finished? There just wasn't enough time in the day. Then my husband came to the rescue with a weekend away for me and my laptop. This is when I realized that we have expectations for the overall goal, but we also have expectations about how every little step along the way will go.

As I left with my laptop, a stack of books and papers, and some bubble bath (always an essential) I realized that both Jim and I held expectations for my time away. It was by these expectations that the success or failure of the weekend would be measured. My contentment and feeling of productivity would be determined by what I "expected" to get accomplished. Jim's satisfaction and determination that his sacrifice (believe me, three days alone with three small children is a sacrifice) was "worth it" would also be determined by his expectations of me.

Let's say I expected to complete one chapter while away, but actually completed two. I would feel great! I would have more than met my expectations and definitely would view the weekend as a success. On the other hand, what if Jim had hoped that I would come home with the book completely done? When I get home and tell him I completed two chapters, he would likely look disappointed and not feel the weekend was "worth it" at all. Look at the very different reactions to the exact same outcome. The end result was that two chapters were completed. But our degree of satisfaction and happiness was very different because of each of our personal expectations.

What I just shared with you is what could have happened had Jim and I not taken time to talk openly about our expectations before I left. Luckily, this is not what occurred. Knowing the impact of expectations on outcome, we did take time to identify our individual expectations for the weekend. This helped us form a more realistic expectation together and therefore avoid the possible disappointments afterward.

## *"Why Don't You Do What I Expect?"*

If expectations are so important to the health of marriage, why are they going unmet in most marriages? There are three possible reasons why we may experience unmet expectations within our marriage. The first is because our spouse was never informed of what our expectations were. This seems to be the number one reason for unmet expectations. How can we meet a need or want or comply with a rule that we don't even know exists? So many couples begin their lives together with stars in their eyes and their thoughts focused on the wedding and honeymoon plans. They spend hours and hours planning the details of what color the cummerbunds should be, or which cake topper to choose. In the process they often miss putting time into planning the most important part of the wedding—the marriage. Couples spend virtually no time discussing their expectations of what life together will be like. Even after years of marriage, we find that most couples are not very good at identifying and discussing their past, present, or future expectations. Disappointments are bound to be present if you don't both know what you expect from yourself or your spouse.

The second possible reason our expectations are not being met may be because we have unrealistic expectations of our marriage and spouse. Many of our spouses would happily meet our needs if they knew what they were and if they were capable of doing so. However, we often want a spouse to do things for us or to take on a role that is completely unrealistic.

The final reason some of our expectations may go unmet is the most destructive of the three. This reason involves your spouse not wanting to meet the expectations you have for your marriage. If you openly state what expectations you have and the two of you evaluate them to be realistic expectations for your relationship, then you should be able to look forward to those expectations being met, at least most of the time. If these realistic expectations are not met, there may be a deeper issue to address with the help of professional counseling.

## *Five Bogus Beliefs of Blissfulness*

Let's look at some of the more commonly held unrealistic expectations or beliefs of marriage. If your expectations are unrealistic, then you can assume that dissatisfaction and unhappiness will be the result if you fail to adjust those expectations.

### *1. This feeling will last forever.*

This belief is often applied to both good and bad feelings. We assume that whatever we feel right now will last forever. Early in our relationships we experience strong positive feelings toward each other. Romance abounds, we get butterflies in our stomach when we see or touch each other, and the world looks beautiful. When we marry, we hold tightly to the belief that this wonderful, enchanting, happy feeling will last forever. It won't.

On the other hand, later in our relationship, negative feelings develop. If these go unresolved, they grow and fester and may capture our total attention. We experience feelings of hurt, anger, and resentment. These negative feelings can be just as strong as the positive feelings we experienced earlier (which by now have been totally wiped from our memory). We begin to believe that this is all we have ever felt or will ever feel. We then assume that these feelings will last forever. They won't. Be careful to keep "feelings" in their proper place and not give them too much power over you. We must remember that feelings do and will change.

### 2. Marriage will solve all my problems.

So many couples today get married for the wrong reasons. They believe marriage is an escape route from the pain and hurts in their lives. Many see marriage as a way to get out of a negative home environment or a means of financial security.

Some may see marriage as a way to solve the relationship problems. This belief is based on the idea that once we get married, everything good will only get better and everything bad will disappear. This is so far from the truth. Actually, marriage may not only not make things all better, it often makes things worse. If the problems were never dealt with and resolved, they will most likely rear their ugly heads again. Why? The "best foot forward" approach to dating is quickly replaced with the "Now I can let my hair down and relax" approach to marriage.

### 3. He or she will make me whole.

When we view marriage as the way to complete ourselves, what are we really saying? That we are not a complete individual on our own and we need someone to make up for what we can't do. This unrealistic expectation is strongly tied to personal struggles of low self-esteem and feelings of inferiority.

The notion of "opposites attract" comes into play. We look for our personal counterpart, the person who will fill in our gaps. We would be much better served to work first on our own self-esteem and learn to accept who we are. Once we are content and comfortable with who we are, then we won't need someone else to make us whole. We will want someone to share our life with but will not need him or her to feel we have a life.

### 4. Marriage will change him or her to be just like me.

This belief is based on the idea that "my way is the best way." We expect our spouse would want to think, feel and act the same way we do. Everyone wants to do things the best way, don't they? And since we are going to think, feel, and act the same way, then of course we must hold the same expectations for our life together. There's really no need to discuss these expectations since we are going to be one in mind, body, and soul. Right? Wrong!

Unspoken rules and unconscious roles of marriage wreak havoc. We must learn to identify and appreciate our differences. In accepting these differences we have the opportunity to grow toward greater intimacy.

### *5. He or she will meet all my needs.*

We believe that Mr. or Mrs. Right is out there and is capable of completely and consistently meeting our every need. We rely on him or her completely. We stop looking to others or ourselves to meet some of our needs. Experiences of caring for our spouse early on may make us feel needed and important; however, if these demands become constant we are likely to begin to feel controlled or suffocated.

We need to reach a healthy balance of dependence and independence, which is called interdependence. The combination of levels of dependence in a relationship is healthy. However, if one member of the couple becomes overly dependent or independent, damage will likely result.

## *Who's on First?*

Have you ever heard your spouse say, "I don't feel important to you!" or maybe, "You are sooooo selfish! Why do you always have to come first?" Or try this one, "You are more interested in your work than you are your family." Statements like these are all tied to how we prioritize. Each one of us will develop a set of priorities that we use (either consciously or unconsciously) to manage our time and resources. These priorities are what help us make both large and small decisions in our daily life. But when developed individually, they will very likely conflict with the priorities of our spouse. This will only make sense when we admit that most of us are beings who like to have things our own way, at least most of the time. When our private priorities, like expectations, are not openly identified and discussed with our spouse, conflict will surely result at some point.

He wants to play golf on his one and only day off. She hopes for a break from the kids.

She wants to get the house cleaned. He's focused on washing the cars.

He works overtime to make some extra money to pay off some

bills. She wants him home in the evening for a family meal.

She wants to put the tax return money in the savings account for a rainy day. He wants to go on a family vacation.

See how easily our different priorities can show up and likely cause conflict in the home? The issue is not usually the right vs. wrong of each of our priorities, but rather the compatibility of them. Learning to identify and evaluate your priorities will greatly increase the likelihood of having a healthy, satisfying relationship.

## Climbing the Ladder of Priorities

I like to look at priorities as rungs on a ladder (a very tall ladder). Everything in our lives occupies one of the rungs, with the top rungs being the most important or pressing at the moment, and the lower rungs being less pressing. For example, at this very moment in time the #1 rung for me is writing this chapter about priorities (#1 for you would be reading it). But my ladder doesn't have only one rung on it. Taking my girls to their dance class might be about rung #6, looking for a new house about #12, and cleaning out the closet somewhere around #187. Everything fits somewhere, and eventually everything gets a chance to occupy the #1 spot. (When I finally get around to cleaning out that closet sometime next century, it will be #1 for at least a moment or two.)

Some things in our lives tend to occupy that coveted #1 spot on a fairly regular basis, and these are the things we need to be identify and evaluate. Those things in your life that occupy the top five rungs of your priority ladder alternate into the #1 position and are therefore the most treasured by you. One way to evaluate what your top five are is to look through your checkbook and your planner. Where we spend our time and our money will often tell us what we treasure. Some of the things that you may find in your top five might include: job, school, children, religion, recreation, spouse, self, cleaning, friends, hobbies, etc. As you identify your priorities, remember that the top five are all fairly equal in their importance to you. In other words, at any given moment, depending on the circumstances, any of these five could take over the #1 position.

Let me give you an example using my own top five list. The top five rungs of my priority ladder include, in no particular order: job, children, marriage, self, and relationship with Jesus. Let's say I am at work and in the middle of a session and I get buzzed telling me the school just called and Taffeta has fallen on the playground and is hurt. My #1 rung, which was occupied by my job, immediately gets replaced and my child becomes #1 as I leave the session to go care for her. Or maybe I am out on a date with Jim and the pager goes off. Again #1 changes quickly, as I move from my spouse to my job this time. And here's a no-brainer, I am actually in the middle of cleaning out that closet that has needed it for the past century and I get a call from a friend inviting me to a movie with the girls. That #187 that had finally made it to #1 is quickly forgotten and "self-time" jumps into #1.

Take a few minutes right now to identify what you believe to be your top five priorities. (The first exercise in the Application section of this chapter will help you do this.) Then it's time to evaluate them. Is there anything there that surprises you? Or maybe more important, is there anything not there that should be? One of the most important things for you as married person is to make sure that both your spouse and yourself are present in the top five. It is not only healthy but also necessary that both you and your spouse rank very highly on each of your lists of priorities in order for the marriage to grow and be satisfying.

Tom and Sheila had been married for nine years. Sheila was three years older than Tom and in her second marriage. She worked full time outside the home and very much loved her two little girls and her husband. She knew that she would do anything for them. She could vaguely remember that she loved reading and jogging, but time for these activities was less available than she wished because of the constant upkeep of the house, fixing meals, and running the kids to their activities. Even if she made plans to go jogging, Tom was often leaving to play golf, so she would have to stay with the children. Or when she planned to read after the kids were in bed, she would fall asleep after just a couple of pages.

Tom also worked full time outside the home. He made good money and enjoyed spending it. He usually spent his days off on the golf course with a buddy, and his vacations hunting with his father and brothers. He provided well for his family and knew that Sheila didn't have to work if she didn't want to. However, he did enjoy the extra income, which allowed him even more financial freedom. He was glad to have married Sheila and he knew his girls were well cared for. She kept the house, cooked for him, and hardly ever nagged. She would periodically blow up about him being gone all the time or about buying a brand new truck without consulting her. But he would simply remind her that he deserved to go out and relax because he worked hard, and he made good money and deserved to enjoy it. She would eventually agree with him and things would be back to normal.

As you read this story, can you see how easily different sets of priorities could have a major impact on a relationship? As Tom and Sheila worked on their top five priorities one of the major problems in their marriage became clear. Sheila had Tom and the children listed in her top five but not herself. Tom, on the other hand, had himself listed but not his children or Sheila. Sheila found herself giving and giving to everyone else to the point that she had nothing left to give to herself. She had difficulty believing that she deserved any time to herself or to be pampered unless everyone else was cared for first (and sometimes she didn't even believe she deserved it then). Although privately she yearned for some time alone, there just didn't seem to be enough of her to go around. And besides, being a good wife and mother meant taking care of everyone else, didn't it? If so, then why did these resentments keep building? Why did she seem to feel less and less satisfied with her marriage as time went on? In large part, because she had never learned the importance of loving herself.

Tom didn't struggle with dissatisfaction in the relationship and seemed very surprised when he found out Sheila wasn't happy. Things were going just fine, weren't they? He was enjoying life for the most part, doing things he enjoyed and spending time with friends and his family. He came home most nights at a decent hour, and he provided well for her and the kids. Sure he felt a little guilty at times, like when he missed seeing his daughter hit her first home run, or when Sheila got upset and called him selfish. But he could usually make up for that by buying her something nice or taking them out for dinner and nothing more would be said for awhile. He thought they were both enjoying life; he knew he was. And he sure thought Sheila was enjoying the time she spent with the children and doing things for him. What more could she want?

As you can see from this example, putting yourself as one of the top five rungs on the ladder and not putting your spouse there means trouble. You are being selfish and focused on what you want. You are not acting as part of the marital team. You are hot-dogging it and grabbing the ball and keeping it for as long as you can to satisfy your own desires.

On the other hand, putting your spouse and children in your top five but not yourself is also unhealthy and can be damaging to the relationship in the long run. Those around you will love it and think you are great for always putting them first. But over time, you will find that you have been doing all the giving and not getting anything (or very little) in return. Eventually the well runs dry and you will have nothing left to give. You find yourself feeling resentful about the giving that you once enjoyed.

As you can plainly see, both expectations and priorities can have a significant impact on your marriage. The more open you can be with yourself and your spouse about what your expectations are and the more you work to have a healthy balance in your priorities, the happier your marriage will be. Here are some exercises to help you and your spouse identify your personal expectations and priorities.

## *Application*

1. *Identify and discuss your expectations.* In this exercise you and your spouse will have a chance to identify the expectations that have been driving your marriage. You may be surprised as some of these surface because many of our expectations we have never even identified ourselves. Using the list of questions at the end of this chapter (and any you can come up with on your own), begin discussing how these relate to you and your marriage. Regardless of how long you have been married, this is an important exercise. Many expectations go unidentified for years and yet are still wreaking havoc on the relationship.

2. *Identify and evaluate your Top Five List.* Using the form below, work to identify the priorities in your life. This is not the time to write down the "right" answer (we all know what "should" be there). This is a time to get very honest with yourself. Where do you really spend most of your time, energy, and money? What do your behaviors identify as being most valuable to you?

After identifying your top five, see if both your spouse and yourself are there. If not, continue down the rungs of the ladder until you both are. How far did you have to go? What does this tell you about changes that need to be made?

Now take a minute to fill out the form for your spouse. What do you see as the major priorities in his or her life?

Once you complete these steps, find some time alone as a couple to discuss each of your lists. Ask your spouse to share with you what they saw as your Top Five. Carefully and lovingly discuss changes that need to be made to bring your priorities into line.

| *My Priority Ladder* | *My spouse's Priority Ladder* |
|---|---|
| 1_____ | 1_____ |
| 2_____ | 2_____ |
| 3_____ | 3_____ |
| 4_____ | 4_____ |
| 5_____ | 5_____ |
| 6_____ | 6_____ |
| 7_____ | 7_____ |
| 8_____ | 8_____ |
| 9_____ | 9_____ |
| 10_____ | 10_____ |

## *Questions to Help Identify Expectations*

1. Who should manage our money?
2. Should we have joint or separate bank accounts?
3. Should the wife work outside the home? Full- or Part-time?
4. Should we have children? How many? When?
5. Should our kids attend public schools, private schools, or be home-schooled?
6. How do we plan to discipline?
7. How should we divide household duties?
8. Should we take family vacations? How often?
9. Where should we spend the holidays?
10. Do we plan to raise our children in church? Which one?
11. How often should we date?
12. How much time do we expect to spend with friends? Family?
13. How much self-time is appropriate?

14. How should we spend our days off work?
15. What was your dad or mom responsible for in your home?
16. What would you do with "extra" money?
17. What is your definition of a wife or husband?
18. How often do you expect to make love?
19. How would you like to spend the evenings?
20. What do you need most from me?
21. How do you expect to fight?
22. How much money do you expect each of us to make?
23. What's your opinion about credit cards?
24. How would you handle a significant tax refund?
25. Where do you want to live?
26. What do you expect our lives to be like in 5, 10, 20 years?
27. Whose career comes first?
28. Would you be willing to move for a job promotion?
29. How can I show you that I love you?
30. What rules did your family have?

# 10

# "It's Never Too Late!"

### Help in Healing Relationships Damaged by Affairs

*A*bove all, love each other deeply,
because love covers over a multitude of sins."
*1 Peter 4:8*

You finally made it to the last chapter (or maybe you skimmed the chapter titles and turned here first). Are you saying to yourself, "Yeah, this all sounds great and would probably work for other marriages, but not mine. I'm really hurting and my marriage is falling apart! We need serious help." This chapter is for you. The principals in this book apply even to highly damaged relationships.

Remember the analogy of marriage as a garden? Maybe your garden is in very bad shape. Maybe your garden has been seriously neglected for a long time. It may be over ridden with weeds to the point that it hardly resembles a garden at all. Or maybe it has been hit by a hailstorm and beaten down to the point that you wonder if it can be salvaged. Regardless of the current condition of your garden, change and healing are possible if both partners are willing to get in and work on it. Change and healing will require an open and sincere commitment to the marriage and patience. Change doesn't come easily or quickly, but it does come.

There are several good books on bookstore shelves now that focus entirely on healing destructive and damaged relationships, including those struggling through an affair. This chapter is only a sampling of suggestions on how to heal your marriage. Also, be aware that these types of relationships often require more than a self-help book. In addition to reading, I encourage you to seek out a trained Christian marriage counselor.

# "Was It Really an Affair?"

This is a question I am asked more often than I care to count. The word "affair" has been used in many contexts and situations but can be difficult to define when it comes to the marital relationship. Before I share with you my definition of an affair, let's take a look at several couples lives and you decide what you think. "Was it really an affair?"

### Couple #1: Sharron and Tim

Sharron and Tim had been married 13 years and seemed more like roommates than lovers. They had three lovely children who seemed to take up 110 percent of Sharron's time and attention. From the first waking moment of the day she turned her attention to the needs of her kids. She prided herself on being a great mom. She took time to talk to her kids and was openly affectionate with them. She knew the importance of letting your children know how much you love them. Sharron was definitely not shy in giving and asking for hugs and squeezes from the kids, but she never seemed to do this for Tim anymore. Tim found himself watching from a distance as she cuddled with their children as they read books or watched a movie together. She always seemed to have a barrier of children around her that he couldn't get through. Although he loved their children just as much as Sharron did, he found himself beginning to resent and even feel jealous of them. He felt she was giving herself more to the children than to him.

### Couple #2: Carrie and Duane

Carrie and Duane had only been married for two and a half years and the relationship had been rocky from the beginning. They dated six months before finding out Carrie was pregnant. They knew they loved each other, but this was not how they wanted to start their life together. They made it through that first year, but not without some major bumps and bruises. Pressures piled up, as did the number of arguments. Eventually they decided to separate in hopes of deciding what their next step should be. Duane moved in with his parents on what he was sure would be a temporary basis. He wanted to start over with Carrie and get it right this time. Carrie, however, seemed more interested in getting together with old friends and going out to the dance clubs. Duane knew how much she loved to dance and tried to be supportive of her time with her friends, but his concerns grew over the next several weeks. He had hoped they would be back together by now. One evening they did finally sit down and talk. Carrie stated her desire to work on the marriage but felt there was something he ought to know. She told him that she had "made a mistake" a couple of weeks before. She admitted to drinking too much, going home with a guy she hardly knew, and sleeping with him. She tried to tell him it was "no big deal" because she had no feelings for him and would probably never see him again. "It just happened, I didn't plan it or anything. And besides, we were separated." If she was right and it really was "no big deal," why did he feel like his heart had just been ripped out of his chest?

### Couple #3: Max and Jeannie

Max and Jeannie had been married 36 years and both had felt they had a fairly good relationship most of that time. Jeannie joined the work force after all the children were out of the house and was enjoying this time for herself. Max, on the other hand, had been retired for two years and loved his free time. He would get up every morning and head to the donut shop where he had coffee and visited with old friends. He developed a friendship with Carol, one of the waitresses, who was playful and flirtatious. He saw this as innocent play at first, but eventually found himself hanging out even after the guys had left just to talk to her. They would often go to lunch together "just to talk." He found himself sharing all kinds of things with her, things he didn't even share with Jeannie. He made sure to tell Jeannie about his lunches with Carol, because he didn't keep secrets from her, and besides, this was just a friend. When Jeannie would voice her concern or seem jealous, Max reassured her there was nothing to be worried about. Jeannie noticed changes in Max's behaviors. He started staying home less and less during the day, and was less available to have lunch with her. When they did get together, his conversations seemed to focus on things he and Carol had done or talked about. She even asked him one day if he was in love or having an affair with Carol because she seemed to be all he thought about. Of course he denied that and said he would never cheat on her. If that were true, why did she feel so hurt?

### Couple #4: Scott and Tamera

Scott and Tamera have been together practically their whole lives.

They grew up in the same small town, lived just a few blocks from each other and attended the same schools. When they started dating it seemed like something fairy tales are made of. They got married out of high school, and Tamera went to work while Scott attended a local junior college. Scott loved their little town and hoped to raise their children there. Although Tamera had always hoped to see more of the world, she was willing to stay put because that's what made Scott happy. As the children came, their roles changed and Tamera began staying home while Scott went off to work every morning. For several years, both seemed satisfied with the life they had chosen — Tamera less so than Scott, however. By the time the children were all in school, Tamera had begun to feel less useful. Her restlessness during the days grew and she began to search out new stimulation, which she soon found on the Internet. As she surfed the Net she realized there was a whole world out there for her to experience from the comfort of her own home. She learned about places she had never been and things she would never do and she began to meet and talk to people from all over the world. This experience became addictive, and there were days she couldn't wait until everyone was gone so she could sign on. She enjoyed her time in the chat rooms the most as she felt herself actually developing friendships with these people she knew she would never see face to face.

One day, after signing on, she received an instant message from SKETER2, a man from one of the chat rooms she often visited. She knew very little about him except that he was four years older than her and from New York City. As they started "talking" she realized how enthralled she was with him and his life. Over the next several weeks, their communications became more and more frequent and more and more private, but only on the computer. She knew not to give out her phone number or even her real name. It was just fun being whoever she wanted to be. Tamera became more involved in talking with SKETER2 until she found herself not wanting to break away to go get the kids at school or staying up late after everyone had gone to bed. Scott had noticed Tamera's apparent obsession with the computer and chat rooms but didn't say anything, because overall she seemed happier and less restless. SKETER2 became more flirtatious, complimentary, and even openly sexual at times. Tamera found herself enjoying this attention and eventually engaging in it as well. Finally it happened: the conversation became totally sexual and Tamera realized what "cybersex" was all about. She was surprised at how aroused she became but discounted it as "just talk." Then one day Scott found an e-mail that was very sexual in nature and accused her of having an affair. She tried to explain that it wasn't what he thought. She didn't even know who SKETER2 really was, and he sure didn't know who she was. They never exchanged phone numbers or planned to meet. They didn't know what each other looked like. "It was just cybersex, that doesn't count as an affair." But regardless of what she said, Scott felt betrayed.

### Couple #5: Steve and Beth

Steve met Beth while he was in college. She worked at the snack bar on campus during the day and attended night classes in cosmetology. He was just in college for the experience. He knew he would be going to work for the family business when he graduated. His dad was already holding a vice-president position just for him. They definitely came from opposite sides of the track. It seemed that these differences actually drew them to each other. After all, opposites do attract, don't they? They eventually married—a real Cinderella story—except for the happily ever after part. Steve taught Beth all the proper things to do and say and loved showing her off at the office parties and business dinners. Beth enjoyed her new lifestyle and was committed to making Steve happy when he was home, which became less and less often. Steve threw himself into the company and tried to explain to Beth that he had to do this at first to "prove himself" to the other officers. He didn't want people to think he got his position just because Dad owned the company. But truth be known, Steve really loved his work and found himself becoming a workaholic. There was always one more thing to do before calling it a day. He knew Beth would have things under control at home and would warm his dinner whenever he got there. He quickly earned the respect and admiration of his coworkers and it was this admiration that seemed to fuel him. When he would try to talk to Beth about the deal he helped salvage or the profit his part of the company was showing, she didn't seem to even hear him. But she would go on and on about his missing their son's soccer game again. She just didn't seem to understand how important he was to the company, but people at work did, and the time he spent with them continued to increase.

### Couple #6: Charles and Edna

Charles was the CEO of a major company and traveled through North America on a regular basis. He had been married to Edna for 20 years and she seemed used to his frequent travel. She spent her time raising two children and in volunteer activities and women's groups. There was no need for her to work because Charles provided quite well for the family and she appreciated that. She did not travel much with Charles because of her need to be available for the children and a fear of flying. Charles seemed to understand that now, although early on in their relationship he would ask her to go many times. They seemed finally to have reached an understanding and didn't discuss it much anymore.

Charles' desire to have a travel companion in part is what led to his relationship with Tonya. Tonya had traveled with him and his partners on several occasions as their coordinator. His relationship with her grew and eventually became sexual. For the past 14 years Charles has felt he had the best of both worlds. A devoted wife at home loving and caring for his children, and a mistress who traveled and gave him "companionship" when he was away from home. He had trouble seeing anything wrong with this situation in a work environment where the men talk just as much about their wives as they do about their girlfriends. It seemed "normal" in his circle of friends. He didn't feel he was hurting either woman because he provided well for both of them and gave them each the part of him he thought they wanted. He wasn't sure if Edna knew about Tonya but he figured she might have some idea and hadn't said anything. He figured she was thankful not to have to worry about flying around the country with him. He often justified the relationship because it didn't really hurt anyone, did it?

# What Do You Think?

How many of these couples are suffering from an "affair"? Two? Three? Maybe even four? Your answer will depend on your personal definition of "affair." In my opinion all six couples are struggling with an affair situation in their marriage.

In my practice I have heard many stories of couples who feel they are suffering from an affair. I have also heard just about as many excuses for why a particular person's behavior does not really count as an affair. Their actions don't really count as an affair because … we never had intercourse … it was only a kiss … I don't even know his name … my wife wasn't meeting my needs in that area … I think I love him, but nothing has happened. On and on the excuses flow. Does having a "really good excuse" justify the hurt and pain? Absolutely not!

When you married, you committed before God to "forsake all others" and allow your spouse to be the first and foremost person to meet your needs. My definition of an "affair" is:

**Anything or anyone that comes between you and your spouse, other than God.**

Willard Harley, in his book *His Needs, Her Needs*[1] has identified what he calls the top five needs of men and the top five needs of women. He proposes that these basic needs must be met. And, if they are not met first and foremost by our spouse we are vulnerable to an affair. For example, one of women's top five needs is the need for affection. For the marriage relationship to be strong and healthy, her husband should be the person she receives her basic requirement of affection from. If for some reason he is not satisfying that need for her, she will begin to seek it from other sources. As with Couple #1 above, she may find herself in an "affair" with her children who are more than happy to hug and snuggle with mom. This is not a sexual or "bad" relationship; it is simply that her need to be touched in a safe, nonsexual, affectionate way is being met by someone other than her husband. Now don't take this to the extreme. All moms love to hug and snuggle with their little ones and that doesn't mean they are having an "affair" with their kids. As long as her husband is the primary source of this need, any additional affection is just wonderful icing on the cake. It only becomes a problem when the husband is not, for whatever reason, meeting that need or when she begins to put the kids in that primary role.

Another example involves one of a man's top five needs being identified as the need for admiration. If his wife does not adequately meet this need, he may seek it in other places. And, like Couple #5, a place many men feel admired is in their work environment. As he strives to do his best for himself and his company, he will likely be praised, promoted, and admired. If the professional environment becomes his primary place for getting his need for admiration met, he may become overly involved and invested in his work environment, thus having an "affair" with his job.

Based on the definition above, each of the six couples described above are actively engaged in some form of an affair. They each struggle with one of the spouses searching for and finding some of their needs outside the marital relationship.

The physical or sexual affair is only one type of affair. There are also affairs of the heart (emotional affairs) which can be just as damaging to the relationship. It's not the type of contact that defines the affair as much as the sense of betrayal. Does your spouse feel hurt and betrayed? Does he or she feel you have given some (any) part of yourself to someone else that should have been saved for him or her alone? You can give from your heart, emotions, mind or body; any of these can involve betrayal and a loss of trust.

## *Let the Healing Begin!*

The healing process has several components. The more of these components are present, the more favorable the prognosis will be for your marriage to remain intact.

*1. Admit and accept the fact that an affair has occurred within your marriage.* "Therefore, confess your sins to each other and pray for each other so that you may be healed" (James 5:16). Both parties tend to reach for denial in the early stages of affair work. The unfaithful spouse may lie if confronted directly or may minimize or justify his or her behaviors. The faithful spouse also may find comfort in denying that their spouse has betrayed them because, "I just can't believe it." He or she may ignore obvious signs or natural intuition, choosing instead to believe this couldn't happen in their marriage. The Bible says in Proverbs 28:13, "He who conceals his sins does not prosper, but whoever confesses and renounces them finds mercy." It is impossible to begin healing as long as we remain in denial. Changes absolutely cannot occur until we are openly aware that there is a problem.

*2. Cut off contact with the "other woman or man" completely at the soonest possible moment.* "The spirit is willing, but the body is weak" (Matthew 26:41). I've watched many marriages begin to heal only to fail again because the "other person" remained in the picture. Cutting off contact with this person can be a difficult component because the majority of affairs do not occur with a total stranger. Rather, an affair happens with someone we know such as a friend, family member, or coworker. If it becomes impossible to cut all contact, strive for the most minimal amount of contact possible, or cut off all contact for at least a set period of time. The more contact allowed with the other person, the more likely it is that the behaviors will repeat themselves.

*3. Enter a time of questioning and honest answers.* "Kings (and spouses) take pleasure in honest lips; they value a man who speaks the truth" (Proverbs 16:13). Get things out in the open. Regardless of how much this may hurt at the moment, it really can help in the long run. When you are ready to move past the hurt of an affair, you both need to feel secure that you know everything you need to know to move forward. The last thing you need is to begin healing, then weeks or months later the other shoe drops and crushes your heart all over again. Do not withhold information at this stage because you fear it would be "too much" for your spouse to handle or that it might "make things worse." What makes things worse is avoiding total honesty. It is not better to piecemeal information out in these situations.

Although questions may arise months or even years later, the majority of this questioning should be done early on. I suggest an "Honesty Session(s)" to my patients where they both agree to give honest answers—no matter how hard—to any question the spouse asks. Both spouses have a chance to question the other since both are working to build a new relationship together.

This is a point where you can begin to reestablish trust. The unfaithful spouse can begin to rebuild trust by giving information and details before being asked, and by elaborating on the questions that are asked. Answering with a simple yes or no or other brief response is likely to only make your spouse feel you are continuing to hide something. The faithful spouse may feel that he or she must ask the exact right question or never know what really happened.

Men tend to first ask, "Did you sleep with him?" Women are more likely to first ask, "Do you love her?" Men generally tend to feel most betrayed by the physical aspects of the affair and women by the emotional aspects of the affair. Therefore, their initial line of questioning will usually fall in those areas. But before it's all over, both usually ask both sets of questions.

*4. Commit to not bring the topic up out of anger.* "Love … keeps no record of wrongs" (1 Corinthians 13:5). Once both you and your spouse feel you have asked all the questions you need to, it is time for a commitment. This is a commitment to not use these events as a weapon against the other. This is not to say that you don't discuss it ever again. Trust can continue to build as communication occurs, just don't bring it up out of anger. If you struggle with thoughts of the affair, you should be able to bring that up to your spouse and ask for help and prayer support. You should never be afraid to talk to your spouse about anything, even the affair. I have heard couples say that one of them needed to talk about it but were afraid to bring it up because the other spouse might not be thinking about it, "so I don't want to make him think about it." Rest assured, the benefits of communicating openly about this far outweigh the possibility of making your spouse think about it. And besides, he or she is probably already thinking about it too.

Each of the partners in the marriage are on different emotional roller coasters once an affair has been disclosed. The unfaithful spouse experiences a downhill slope of relief and is ready to put all this behind and move on. He or she doesn't want to rehash it. However, the betrayed spouse is just beginning the uphill struggle of becoming aware of the events and needs to talk about it in order to move on. One more way to rebuild trust is for the unfaithful spouse (the one who doesn't want to talk about it) to bring up the topic. By volunteering information, sharing feelings and struggles, and asking how the other is doing in dealing with all this, you show compassion and concern. Doing this is contrary to your natural desire to avoid the topic and therefore shows additional effort on your part to keep communication open and your spouse moving forward.

*5. Be accountable.* "And from each man, too, I will demand an accounting for the life of his fellow man" (Genesis 9:5). For healing to occur and trust to be rebuilt, the unfaithful spouse must be willing to be accountable for his or her activities and whereabouts. Due to the amount of deception that goes into an affair, the betrayed spouse will be suspicious and distrusting about even the littlest things. As the unfaithful spouse, you must be willing to work to rebuild trust. This will likely include being questioned about your day, where you've been, what you did, and who you saw. You will likely be asked to hand over the pager, cell phone, and the bills associated with these for inspection. You may receive unexpected phone calls or visits to your office to confirm you are where you say you are. Accept all of these behaviors and understand them as necessary for awhile as your spouse is healing and the two of you rebuild trust. The more information you volunteer, the more you hold yourself accountable, and the more understanding you are of these behaviors from your spouse, the more trust builds. Eventually the betrayed spouse must begin to allow himself or herself to believe the other spouse for trust to reestablish.

*6. Forgive.* "Bear with each other and forgive whatever grievances you may have against one another. Forgive as the Lord forgave you" (Colossians 3:13). It's time to talk about what I consider one of the hardest stages in the healing process—forgiveness. When you ask newly married couples or couples who have never dealt with an affair if they would be willing or able to forgive their spouse for cheating, you would hear a resounding "No way! I could never forgive that!" But the fact is many couples, once faced with a major betrayal, are willing to try to work things out. And a big part of working things out is being able to eventually reach a point of forgiveness. And that is exactly where many couples hit a major roadblock to their progress.

I believe that people often have difficulty forgiving because they believe forgiveness to be something that it is not. Let's consider what forgiveness is not in order to help better understand what forgiveness is.

Forgiveness is not amnesia. Forgiving and forgetting are different acts. Although God is capable of forgiving and forgetting, we as humans definitely do not excel in this area. Once something is in our minds, especially something painful, it is often difficult to completely forget that it ever happened. Forgiveness must be given even in the face of remembering. Forgiveness enables us to begin to forget by avoiding the constant rehashing of the event in our minds.

Forgiveness is not acquittal. In other words, forgiveness does not mean that the person is blameless and without responsibility. When we recognize the individual as responsible for the hurt he or she has caused, we can reach a point of forgiveness. God forgives us after we have identified that we have done something wrong, taken responsibility for it, and asked for His forgiveness. Can you imagine going to God and saying "I didn't really do anything wrong, but please forgive me anyway." Forgiveness also does not mean that the slate is wiped completely clean. Even with forgiveness, there is still damage to repair and consequences to work through.

Forgiveness is not an award. You cannot earn forgiveness, although many an unfaithful spouse has attempted to. You can never behave or perform "good enough" to earn forgiveness. Forgiveness is freely given without regard for merit.

Forgiveness is not approval. When we forgive, we are not telling our spouse that we approve of what he or she did. If we approved of what they did there would be no need for forgiveness in the first place. Many people get stuck here and think that if they forgive they are saying "it's okay." This seems to come from a response I hear people give all the time. When a child does something wrong, you teach your child to say, "I'm sorry for what I did wrong." Then how do you respond? You likely reach down, give a hug and say "It's okay." Maybe a better response would be "I agree with you that what you did was wrong and I am choosing to forgive you." Forgiveness is saying "No, it's not okay, but I'm choosing to forgive you anyway."

Forgiveness is not acquiescence. It is not permission to go on and do as one pleases or to stay the same. I've often heard the betrayed spouse say, "If I forgive, he will stop trying and just go back to the way things were." Forgiveness is not permission to stay the same, but rather inspires change. Forgiveness is given in the face of knowledge that the future may not be different, but also with the enabling hope that it will. (Excerpts from *Practical Psychology for Pastors*.[2])

*7. Begin to identify and meet each other's needs.* "Hope deferred makes the heart sick, but a longing fulfilled is a tree of life" (Proverbs 13:12). You've identified the affair and asked all your questions. You've cut off contact with the other person. You've forgiven and begun to rebuild trust. Now what? Now you are finally at the place the two of you should have been before the affair ever began.

Affairs often result out of unmet needs within the marriage. I am not condoning marital affairs or taking away the personal responsibility of the unfaithful spouse. The faithful spouse did not "make you do it." The unfaithful one is still responsible and accountable for his or her choice to engage in an affair. However, for healing to be complete, both partners need to evaluate their own needs and determine whether or not they are meeting each other's needs. Talk about this and clearly reveal any unmet needs. So often I have seen couples healing from affairs and one spouse saying to the other "I didn't know you needed that from me."

It is now time to evaluate where the weakness in your marriage came from. What needs do you have that should be met first and foremost in your marriage, and how well is your spouse meeting those needs? Perhaps you have some needs your spouse has always met well. Be sure to share those. It's always nice to hear when we are doing something right. It's likely you have a few needs that your spouse has not adequately met. Work to figure out what those are and to help your spouse learn to meet them for you. A popular notion that I have heard is that people who have affairs aren't getting enough at home. Actually we should consider that they weren't giving enough at home. The driving force of most affairs is not sex. Actually, the driving force is far more powerful than sex. Affairs are much more tied to open conversation and affection and especially a feeling of love and acceptance that is a result of positive time spent together. Doesn't that sound like something we've heard before? Oh, yes, warm fuzzies. Affairs take time and attention to develop and sustain, as do marriages. If the unfaithful spouse was giving as much time, attention, affection, compliments, etc., to the spouse as he or she was to the affair, I'm sure the marriage would be stronger, healthier, and more satisfying for both. If we can focus on remaining "in love" within our marriages then we will not need to look elsewhere for "love."

Spend time with your spouse and get to know each other's needs. Then actively engage in meeting those needs. As the verse at the beginning of this section shows, a longing (need) fulfilled will bring life to your marriage. Encourage each other daily and reevaluate how the two of you are doing often. Use the skills taught in this book to regain the sense of being "in love" and growing a healthier, stronger marriage "till death do you part."

# Endnotes

## Chapter 2: Warm Fuzzies and Cold Pricklies

1 I am thankful to the faculty of the Psychology and ABSED Departments of Oklahoma State University, who's insight and wisdom regarding marriage and family therapy taught me a variety of theories and techniques that have stayed with me and blended over-time to help form my current working theories. It is their knowledge and experience that they shared with me and many students that is sprinkled throughout this book.

## Chapter 3: Worth Your Weight in Gold

1 My theories and opinions regarding the power of feelings and how to change them has been greatly influenced by the clinicians from Burrell Behavorial Health, Springfield, Missouri. I thank them for mentoring me and sharing with me their combined knowledge.

## Chapter 4: How Do I T.R.E.A.S.U.R.E Thee? Let Me Count the Ways

1 http://www.mentalhelp.net/psyhelp/chap10. Article by Clayton E. Tucker-Ladd; "Learning to communicate differently requires practice."
2 *New Webster's Dictionary of the English Language, College Edition* (New York: Consolidated Book Publishers, 1975), 1278.

## Chapter 5: "Honey, Are You Listening?"

1 Robert W. Bly, "Improving Your Listening Skills" (Dumont, NJ: Center for Technical Communication) Internet article; http://espeakonline.com/Cepart1html.
2 McKay, Davis & Fanning, 1983. As referenced on Mental Health Net & CMHC Systems (1995-1999), Internet article, "Listening and Empathy Responding".
3 H. Norman Wright, *Communication: Key to Your Marriage* (Ventura, Calif.: Regal Books, 1974), 55.

## Chapter 6: "Let's Talk"

1 Adapted from John Powell, *Why Am I Afraid to Tell You Who I Am?* (Chicago: Argus Communications, 1969), 54–62.

2 Adapted from Thomas Gordon's book, *P.E.T., Parent Effectiveness Training; The tested new way to raise responsible children* (New York: Plume, 1970), 108–114.

3 Ibid., 108–114.

## Chapter 7: "And the Winner Is ..."

1 John Gottman, *Why Marriages Succeed or Fail: And how you can make yours last* (New York: Simon & Schuster Trade, 1994), 173.

2 Markman, Stanley, & Blumberg, *Fighting for Your Marriage: Positive steps for preventing divorce & preserving a lasting love* (San Francisco: Jossey-Bass, 1994), 38.

## Chapter 8: "For Your Eyes Only"

1 Suggested resources: Dennis Rainey, *Lonely Husbands, Lonely Wives: Rekindling intimacy in every marriage* (Dallas: Word Publishing, 1989), 255. Gary Smalley, *Making Love Last Forever* (Dallas: Word Publishing, 1996). Jimmy Evans, *Marriage on the Rock: God's design for your dream marriage* (Tulsa, Okla.: Vincom, Inc., 1992). Jay Kesler, *Is Your Marriage Really Worth Fighting For?* (Elgin, Ill.: David C. Cook Publishing Co., 1989).

## Chapter 10: "It's Never too Late!"

1 Harley, Willard, *His Needs, Her Needs: Building an Affair Proof Marriage* (Grand Rapids, Mich.: Fleming H. Revell, 1994).

2 Miller and Jackson, *Practical Psychology for Pastors* (Englewood, NJ: Prentice Hall Publishers, 1985).